READ AT YOUR OWN RISQUE!

A Treasury of America's 200 Most Offensive Adult Humor Classics

By
Ted Pincus

*Do not read this book: if you have a history of any allergies related to socially embarrassing terminology; or a history of hypersensitivity related to scatological filth, earthy mirth, or culturally offensive references. Take only at full strength and if convulsive symptoms occur, consult your urologist immediately.

© Copyright 2008, Ted Pincus

All Rights Reserved.

No part of this book may be reproduced, stored in a retrieval system, or transmitted by any means, electronic, mechanical, photocopying, recording, or otherwise, without written permission from the author.

ISBN: 978-1-60388-115-9
1-60388-115-8

Published by Jones Harvest Publishing Co.

PREFACE

Other than the orgasm, what generates as powerful an explosion within the human body as the laugh? I don't mean a minor guffaw or a giggle. I mean a seismic eruption that begins deep in the lungs and soars through the larynx, floods the eyes and climaxes with screams that become gasps. Is there any better excruciating potion for the human spirit?

You and I have had these rare highs at memorable moments of our lifetime. If you're like me, you treasure them.

What produces them? Not pratfalls, or gags, or clever one-liners. Only one thing can usually create those moments. That thing is The Story. Not any old Story. The indigenously American Socially Incorrect Story, which was born long before the term "socially incorrect."

The Adult Story is not a mere joke, nor a slapstick scene in a musical play or film or TV sketch. The Story is a vignette, a sardonic observation of the farces and foibles of our society. It is a ludicrous piece of essential folklore of urban professional culture, a scatological, insulting reflection of our times. It is a tale designed to be offensive and it draws its biting humor from that shock value. It isn't created to hurt and almost never originates out of malice. Usually, the laughter-producing sting element is a reminder of our own inadequacies, rubbing salt into our secret wounds. In a word, The Story is priceless.

But this national treasure is a vanishing species. In the history of the printed word – from Gutenberg to Google – almost every form of human communication has been recorded for posterity. But in the annals of mankind, there's one product that stands alone – so uniquely ephemeral and elusive that it has never been truly contained. Like a capricious spark, The Story has floated around our society traveling only on spoken word, preserved only by a thin verbal thread. Think about one you love – and where did it go? Depending on its flakey lifetime, The Story has an existence that can be extinguished by pure forgetfulness or sustained indefinitely like chain letter on the lips of its carriers.

I have resolved to prevent that extinction. After cataloging many hundreds of Stories worth retelling over five decades, I've selected 200 that I personally rate as classics that warrant preserving and perpetuating at any cost. As with any socially incorrect American Story, no reader will completely agree with my sense of humor or taste. In fact, most of these Stories – by their very nature – are inherently offensive to somebody somewhere. Exaggerated irreverence – the basis of The Story – tickles one person's funny bone while grating upon the next person's sensibilities. Whether earthy to extreme or overstepping political correctness on religious on racial grounds, The Story is destined to offend. And yet, any attempt to sanitize would perpetuate a destructive dilution. To be truly preserved for appreciation by future generations, it must be – like sex or cognac – taken at full strength.

Thus I ask that you not be merely a reader, but a carrier. Join this Comedy Conservation Crusade and spread the gospel.

In my 50 years of studying and cataloging the American Socially Incorrect Story, I've generally found a pattern whereby the best humor is self-inflicted. Jewish customs or deprecation of Jewish characteristics are the key ingredients in The Jewish Story, originated by Jews. The pattern is similar among the Irish, the gays, the blacks, and even among Polish Americans – contrary to the popular perception that they are the butt, rather than the originator, of The Polish Story.

My fascination and love of The Story turned me into a compulsive collector at an early age. And as a professional communicator, I've spent the better part of a lifetime witnessing the emergence of this truly special 20th Century American communications form, living and working at the primary source: Wall Street and the nation's other investment centers – like LaSalle Street and Montgomery Street – in the corporate executive suite, and in the newsrooms.

Regardless of the origin or the dialectician skills of the teller, certain features of The Socially Incorrect Story are unique.

First is its singular ability to produce more profound, uncontrolled laughter than virtually any other humor form.

Second is its ability to utterly overwhelm and devastate – in the positive sense – any gathering of hip, aware human beings. A truly good new Story can instantly electrify, awaken and enliven the group with collective joy as few other things can.

Third is its magical ability to spread seemingly even faster than the speed of sound. It can race through a cocktail gathering or a brokerage office within minutes and like some wild epidemic, it can travel coast to coast and back again with miraculous speed. For many years, this happened by phone, then fax. Nowadays, email has become the network of choice.

Fourth is its uncannily accurate reflection of the times and our secret sentiments regarding shifts in the human condition. It punctures holes in the pompous, stings the sanctimonious, and gleefully performs a sacrilege on things that have been sacred for perhaps too long.

Therefore do I ask in advance that any reader of this collection extract what he or she can in entertainment value, and view the remainder as an academic examination of one of our civilization's unique social phenomena, forgiving the offensive specimens that do indeed appear in unvarnished form.

Caveat lector.

DEDICATION

To my wife, Sherri, whose spirit is the quintessence of humor and humanity.

ACKNOWLEDGEMENTS

Special deepest thanks to these enthusiasts who have been either primarily originators, distributors or avid carriers.

Bea Bahr, Ben Behr, Bill Braman, Don Frisch, Ethel Gofen, Milt Gilbert, Jim Goldman, Esther Hiller, Bob Katz, Stan Katz, Ira Kaufman, Syd Lilly, Cy Mager, Bob Mann, Frank Nash, Marshall Ruchman, Sid Salinger, Carol Scott, Lee Shull, Mike Schwimmer, Steve Sehler.

CONTENTS

CHAPTERS

1. PROMISCUITY — You've Been a Bad Girl. Go to my Room 1
2. INGENUITY — A Mind is a Terrible Thing to Taste 24
3. GLOBETROTTING — Give us Another Rendition 42
4. THE ANIMAL KINGDOM — Robbing PETA To Pay All 56
5. FATEFUL ENCOUNTERS — It's Been Nice No-ing You 77
6. LIFE'S DEVASTATING MOMENTS — Personal Crisis Management is an Art Form 90
7. SPORTS — The Enthusiastic Athletics Supporter 106
8. MEDICINE — Here's to the Hype-and-Critical Oath 120
9. PROFESSIONALISM — Expertise is in the Eye of the Beholden 137
10. WEDDINGS — Wipe That Loehengrin Off Your Face 149
11. MARRIAGE — Two's a Crowd 159
12. CHILDREN — I Kid You Not! 183
13. THE CLERGY — Torah! Torah! Torah! And Crucifixations ... 195
14. GERIATRICKS — Older.Bolder.Better.Wetter. 208
15. AFTERLIFE — Getting to Heaven Isn't Rocket Séance 236

CHAPTER ONE

PROMISCUITY

You've Been A Bad Girl. Go To My Room.

1.   FALSE FACE, SCHMALTZ FACE

"Don't get excited, Bernie, the costume isn't much," Blanche says sleepily.

"Well, you better get your ass moving, because it's almost party time," Bernie yells.

"You know what, Bernie? I've got a splitting headache and I think I'm going to take a pass. Go ahead and go without me and enjoy!"

"What? Are you sure? You actually want me to do this thing without you, honey?" Bernie says. "You mean, without even seeing you in your new costume?"

"Yep, that's just what I mean. Go and enjoy, have a great time. Leave me in peace."

Shrugging his shoulders, Bernie puts the finishing touches on his costume and heads for the car. He arrives at the totally masked party as a solo performer and as a masked, dashing Zorro, he heads straight for all of the available damsels at the affair. Between boozing and schmoozing, he's having the time of his life.

Meanwhile, an hour later, Blanche miraculously finds that her headache has vanished. Not only does she decide to go to the affair after all and show off her new costume and mask, but a sneaking suspicion tells her that this would be a unique opportunity to attend a party incognito and spend the first few minutes observing what her playboy husband does at a social affair when she's not present. Since she'll enter on a completely anonymous basis, in an attire and mask that no one has ever seen, including her husband, it would be an unprecedented opportunity!

Reviving herself quickly, she dons her new attire and mask, and takes the second car and drives over to the party.

Upon entering the ballroom, Blanche is stunned to see her wayward husband humping and bumping every comely damsel on the dance floor. After watching this performance for several minutes, she resolves to take the plunge. Resolutely, she strolls out onto the dance floor and cuts in.

Throwing her body into her masked Zorro, and disguising her voice, Blanche whirls him around and drives him to a frenzy of passion. Finally, she whispers in his ear, "Hey, big boy, why don't we head for my car and have the rest of this dance on the back seat?" Her partner readily complies, the two head for the parking lot and a wild tryst ensues. Without once removing her mask, Blanche has an ecstatic time, completes the escapade, bids her partner good night, he leaves and she immediately drives home.

Two hours later, Bernie arrives home, enters the bedroom and Blanche is already sound asleep. Opening one eye, she murmurs, "Bernie, is that you? How was the party?"

"Dullsville," says her husband. "You didn't miss anything. In fact, I spent the last half of the evening having scotches and shooting pool with the boys in the back room. But do you wanna hear a wild story? You'll never guess what happened to the guy who borrowed my Zorro costume!"

2. AGE OF ENLIGHTENMENT.

It's almost midnight when a policeman is patrolling a lonely city park. As he motors up a secluded park drive, he sees a single auto parked at the far end of a small parking lot. Its lights are off. The policeman drives up to the parked car and shines his light in the window. Lo and behold, he sees the face of a young man, obviously intent on reading by flashlight. The policeman leaves his car, walks over and shines his flashlight through the driver's side window and motions that the window be rolled down. The young man complies.

"Exactly what are you doing, fella?" the policeman says.

"I'm reading *TIME Magazine*, Officer," says the young man. Suddenly, the policeman shines his light into the rear seat of the car, seeing a beautiful young woman intently knitting a sweater.

"And what about her?" the policeman inquires.

"Officer, she's doing exactly what it looks like – she's knitting herself a new sweater."

"OK, young man, let me see your license," says the policeman. The young man hands the license to the cop. "Hmm, OK, so I see you're 25. And what's her age?"

"Officer, in 11 minutes, she'll be 18."

3. INTRODUCTION TO TELECOM.

A middle-aged business man from Wichita checks into Chicago's Four Seasons Hotel. He has a satisfying dinner and retires to his room. At about 11:30 p.m. he's reading a local magazine, when he notices on the rear cover an incredibly voluptuous blonde with a beckoning eye, and a caption below saying, "Why not call me?" Below the caption is a local phone number.

He ponders the situation a while longer, he studies the rear cover for a good half hour, then impulsively leans over and picks up the telephone and dials.

A voice answers, "Hello?"

"Honey," he murmurs, "my name's Jack and I'm in room 1921 at the Four Seasons Hotel. I'm staring at your photo and am getting hotter by the minute. Get your ass over here, knock on my door, The minute I open it, I'm gonna pull you in here, rip all your clothes off and I'm gonna fuck your brains out in every position known to anthropology. What do you think of that?"

"I think that sounds great," says the feminine voice, "but to get an outside line, you have to first dial 9."

4.   FATHERLY LOVE.

Excitedly, James races into the hospital and into his wife's maternity room.

"Is dis excitin'! Where's dat baby?"

"Right here, James, have a look. Isn't she beautiful?"

James stands there stupefied. He grimaces. "Wait a minute, honey. Wait a minute! Somethin's wrong. Dis can't be mah baby! Dis has to be the ugliest baby on the planet! I've never seen a uglier child!"

"Oh, James, how can you say dat? Of course dis child is ours."

"Impossible, honey! Look at our two grown, beautiful daughters. This one can't possibly be mine. Hey, baby, have you been playin' around on me?"

She smiles sweetly and says, "Not this time."

5. ADVANCED VOCABULARY.

Horace comes home to his second floor walkup apartment and finds to his dismay that all of his furniture and belongings are out on the landing. He finds the door locked with a newly installed lock. He pounds on the door and screams, "Hey, Margie, what are you doing? All of my stuff is out here on the landing!"

From inside, a young female voice yells, "We're through, Horace, we're through. You're out of here! Take your stuff and go!"

"Why? Why?"

"Because the whole neighborhood is talking! Everybody says you're a pedophile!"

"Wow, Margie, that's a big word for a ten-year-old!"

6. PATERNAL COUNSEL.

Pinocchio is sitting in the carpentry shop of his father, the kind old Geppetto. The young boy puppet says "I got a problem. Pop, my dilemma is that my girlfriend hates splinters. She gets lots of them when we make love. What can I do?"

"Well, my son, my best advice is for you to work on it with a little sandpaper." A week goes by. Finally one day at breakfast, Geppetto says to Pinocchio, "Well, son, how's the girlfriend?"

"Pop, who needs girlfriends?"

7. TREBLE SCREENING.

Socrates is strolling through the Roman Forum when a friend suddenly races up to him.

"Socrates! Socrates! I have news for you, important news!"

"Wait, my friend, wait," says Socrates. "You know very well that I never waste time listening to trivia. Every piece of news I receive must pass my triple filter. First, it must be useful. Is this news useful?"

"Well, Socrates, I'm not sure. I'm just not really sure if this news is useful."

"Well, let's see if it passes the second test. Is it truthful?"

"Well, Socrates," says the friend, "I think so. I think it's truthful, but I can't be absolutely sure."

"All right," says Socrates, "let's see about the third test. It must be honorable. Is this news honorable?"

"Honestly, Socrates, I can't say that it is."

"In that case," says Socrates, "I don't wanna hear it. Be gone with you."

And that is why Socrates never knew that Plato was banging his wife.

8. THE ALIBI.

Mrs. Rosenwald is in her bedroom on the second floor of her suburban home, having a marvelous afternoon tryst with her lover. Suddenly, she hears a noise and freezes.

"Oh, my God! I think I hear my husband! Why in the world is he home so early! Quick! You've got to hide! Get in that clothes closet quickly!"

The lover immediately jumps, nude, out of bed and races to the closet, closing the door behind him. He dives through an entire curtain of her husband's suits and stands there motionless, sandwiched between a blue gabardine and a grey herringbone.

The husband comes upstairs, enters the bedroom, says hello to his wife and suddenly spots someone else's socks on the floor. Instantly suspicious, his face turns sinister and he begins to slowly inspect the entire bedroom in search of more clues. He suddenly swings open the closet door, flips on the light and steps inside. It isn't long before he throws back a row of suits and sees the lover standing stiffly at full attention, staring forward with a weak smile.

"And just who the fuck are you?" says the husband, in a rage.

Speechless for a moment, the lover finally musters the best smile he can and says in a matter-of-fact tone, "I'm the moth inspector."

"The moth inspector! The moth inspector!" screams the husband. "You're standing there stark naked!"

"I know. I guess I got here too late."

9. PICTURE THIS.

A young fellow picks up a girl in a bar. They go back to her apartment and make love.

Laying on the bed exhausted, the young fellow turns and notices a handsome male in a large photograph on the dresser.

"Gee, I didn't notice that before," he says. "Is that your boyfriend?"

"No, that's me before the operation."

10.   THE IDEAL WOMAN.

Guido is sitting in a bar with his friend, Luigi. Suddenly, his friend Luigi turns to him and says, "Guido, do you like a-women with a-pocmarked a-face?"

"No, Luigi, I don't."

"Guido, do you like a-women with a-tits a-sagging down to her a-navel?"

"No, Luigi, I don't."

"Guido, do you like a-women with lots of a-hair under her arms and a mustache on her lip?"

"No, Luigi, I don't."

"Then Guido, why are you fucking my wife?"

11. BATHHOUSE GOSSIP.

Aki enters his luxurious penthouse near downtown Tokyo. After pouring himself a saketini, he strolls into the bedroom and confronts his wife.

"Moriko-san, I have heard some very disturbing rumor. Word has it that you are seeing an American."

"No, Aki-san!"

"It is my understanding, Moriko-san, that this American is a doctor."

"No, Aki-san!"

"Mariko-san, I understand that this man is a Jewish-American doctor!"

"Aki-san...where are you hearing all this michigas?"

12. TURNABOUT

In New York, a Park Avenue matron is enjoying a matinee tryst in bed with her lover.

Suddenly, her cell phone rings on the bed stand and she reaches for it.

"Hello. Oh, it's you! How are you, darling? How's everything going? Are you eating well? Is the weather good…oh, that's wonderful! Marvelous. Well, everything's just great here. Stay dry, honey, get lots of sleep, and hurry back."

She clicks the phone off, rolls over and whispers to her lover, "That was Irv. He says he's having a fabulous time on his fishing trip with you."

13. ULTIMATE SACRIFICE.

Herschel and Hortense are celebrating their 50th wedding anniversary. They're having champagne and dinner by candlelight. They toast each other and their half-century romance and are deep in reminiscence.

Herschel finally interrupts with a change of subject. "You know, Hortense, we've been married 50 years and I've never really asked you one important question."

"What's that, my darling?"

"Well, have you ever been unfaithful to me?"

"Well, Herschel, after 50 years, I guess I can answer that question truthfully. Yes, I have – but always with your best interests at heart."

"How many times, Hortense?"

"Three, my dear."

"Three times? What were they?"

"The first time, Herschel, was that year when your business was on the rocks. You weren't sure you were going to make it. We were both afraid it was going to go under. Remember? And remember that night that we invited the banker over for dinner? You know, the one whose loan we needed so desperately."

"Hortense, you mean…you mean you did that to save my business? Really?" She nodded. "And when was the next time?"

"The next time, darling, was when you needed that coronary bypass surgery and we decided to try to find the very best surgeon in the world and we went all the way to Houston to convince Dr. DeBakey to do the surgery personally."

"You mean…you mean you actually did that to save my life?" Again, she nodded. "And when was the third time?"

"Darling, do you remember when you were running for president of the congregation…and you were 47 votes short?"

14. THE DOWN ELEVATOR.

A world-famous rock star stepped out of his penthouse apartment in a high-rise building in Beverly Hills. Alone in the elevator at the 50th floor, he watches the numbers descend to 45. The door opens and a sweet young damsel enters the car. She takes one look at him and melts.

"Oh, my God!" she whispers. "Is it really you? Is it?" she asks .

"Yes, it's me. It's really me," the rock star acknowledges to the bright-eyed teenybopper.

"Oh, wow! I mean, wow! This is the most exciting moment of my life. I mean, like…do you think…we have many floors before the street level, and we're here alone in the elevator, just the two of us. Do you think, like, it would be too much to ask if I could very, very quickly unzip your fly and take out your manhood and give you one minute of oral sex?"

The rock star stands there contemplating. After a moment of deep thought, he says, "Well…I guess so…but what's in it for me?"

15. LIFE IS A JOURNEY.

Norbert and Manny are two sperm, swimming along desperately in the darkness.

"Norbert!" says Manny, "this is so exciting! Do you think we're approaching the uterus?"

"Hell no, Manny! We haven't even passed the esophagus yet!"

16. RODEO FORNICATION.

"Did you know that they now have a new event called Rodeo Fornication?"

"No, how is it played?"

"Well, the contestant places his wife facedown in bed and mounts her from the rear. He then places his left hand upon her left breast and grasps it tightly. He then leans down and whispers into her ear, 'Honey, this is the way my lover likes it!' Then he tries to hang on for ten seconds!"

17. EXECUTIVE A.W.O.L.

Recently, Fensterwald notices that his boss leaves the office quite early. In fact, lately he has been leaving at precisely 2 p.m. every day.

Fensterwald confides to his office pal, Schminter, "You know, Schminter, old buddy, this is becoming my golden opportunity. The weather is fabulous, and I've been dying to get in more golfing time. I think I'm going to take a chance and head for the golf course every afternoon that the boss takes off."

And that's just what he does. Each day at exactly 2:30, Fensterwald slips out of the office, climbs in his car, golf bag stowed nicely in the trunk, and heads for a suburban golf course where he can play to his heart's content, undetected.

One afternoon, however, Fensterwald decides to switch plans and give his wife a little surprise. He drives up his street and is about to turn into his driveway, only to find the boss's care parked there. He glances at his house and notices that the master bedroom shades are pulled. He gulps, floors the accelerator and zooms off down the street. The next morning, he confronts Schminter at the water cooler. His face is ashen white, and he whispers, "Wow, Schminter, you'll never guess what happened yesterday. I think I'm going to give up on this whole idea of playing hooky and sneaking in afternoon golf!"

"How come, Fensterwald?"

"Well, I had a close one yesterday. I almost got caught!"

18.   MIGRAINE IS WORSE THAN YOUR GRAIN.

A man approaches his coworker at the office water cooler. "Fred, what's the matter?"

"Oh Klaus, it's really awful. I just keep getting these tremendous migraine headaches and I can't get rid of them!"

"What have you tried, Fred?"

"Klaus, I've tried everything. Nothing seems to work."

"Well, Fred, I've got a sure-fire solution. I used to get bad migraines all the time. And whenever it happened, I would go home and I would kneel down on the floor and put my head between my wife's thighs. She has some very strong thigh muscles, and she applies a lot of pressure to my temples with her thighs. I keep my head there under that pressure for about ten minutes and at the end of that time, my headache is completely disappeared and it doesn't come back."

"Gee, that's fabulous, Klaus. Thanks for the tip. I'll have to try it."

Three days pass before Klaus sees Fred again in the office corridor. "Well, Fred, how are you doing? Did you try my solution?"

"Yes, Klaus, it's a terrific remedy. I tried it and it worked perfectly – and by the way, you've got a gorgeous apartment!"

19. CHALK TALK.

Herman is a mild-mannered accountant who leads a life of pure routine. Part of that routine is to take the same bus home from the office every day at exactly 5:30 p.m. He's been doing it for many, many years.

But today is going to be different. Herman sits down in his usual seat on the bus and begins to read his newspaper, and all of a sudden out of the corner of his eye, he notices an absolutely incredibly stunning young redhead who sits down next to him and crosses her legs. When she accidentally brushes his arm, Herman starts to become slightly agitated. When she then starts up a conversation with him, his pulse rate steadily quickens. Within five minutes, the aggressive little thing has captivated her prey. Within another ten minutes, she induces him to get off the bus at her stop, walk a short distance to her apartment, pour some cocktails, have some dinner, hop into bed and there she gives him the time of his life for an entire evening. He finally dozes off.

It's now 7 a.m. and Herman walks up in a cold sweat. Visions of his wife, dinner still waiting on the table since last night, and a scene of likely violence fill his fevered brain. His imagination stretches for a solution in desperation.

Suddenly, he swings his legs out of bed, sits on the edge and says to his lovely companion, "Quick! Quick! Find me some chalk." The young redhead grins, trying to imagine some new kinky scene that her partner is about to concoct. Eager to cooperate, she runs off to the next room to find the chalk. Meanwhile, Herman frantically puts on his shirt, tie, shorts, socks, shoes and business suit. His companion finally returns with the chalk. Herman sits on the edge of the bed and says, "Now, quick, cover my hands with chalk." She complies with his directions, still wondering what he's up to.

With his hands covered light in chalk dust, he gives her a quick peck of farewell on the cheek, along with a major thank you and dashes off to the bus stop. He catches the next bus homeward and arrives back at his own apartment 15 minutes later. As he quietly creeps into the house, there is his wife standing on the staircase, fuming.

"Okay, Sadie, okay, I can understand that you're upset. I can explain everything. Here's my confession. When I left the office last night, I fully intended to come home to dinner the same as always. But suddenly, I found an incredibly gorgeous young redhead sitting next to me on the bus. She was enormously attracted to me, and she kept after me and after me, and finally induced me to get off the bus at her stop and go back to her apartment where she quickly seduced me, and I spent the rest of the evening fucking my brains out."

Sadie stands there with her hands on her hips, a skeptical grimace across her face. She squints at Herman's clenched fists as he quivers there in the foyer before her.

"Herman! Let me see those hands!" she commands. Meekly, sheepishly, Herman unclenches his fists and obediently displays the palms of his hands to his angry mate.

"I thought so! You bastard!" screams Sadie. "You lying son-of-a-bitch! You've been out bowling with the boys all night!"

20. THE ULTIMATE DEFINITION OF SAVOIR FAIRE.

Three Frenchmen are sitting around a bistro table discussing the definition of *savoir faire*.

The first one states, "You know, mon amis, to mee zee most graphic definition of *savoir faire* would be zee occasion in which a man returns home from the zee office, opens zee front door, sees another man's shoes in zee front hall, hears some suspicious sounds from zee second floor, shrugs his shoulders and strolls into zee kitchen and pours himself a glass of Beaujolais. Zat is *savoir faire*!"

His friends nod agreement, but then the second gentleman in the group states: "Oui, mon amis, zat is very close to a perfect definition. But not quite. True *savoir faire* would be zis: Zee man comes home from zee office, opens zee door, sees another man's shoes in zee front hall, zen slowly walks up zee stairs, opens zee bedroom door, and sees his wife in bed with another man. With a wave of his hand, he says, 'Proceed, sil vous plait!' Zat is true *savoir faire*!"

The other two men nod assent, but the third raises his finger. "Just a moment, mon amis. I agree – but not quite! True *savoir faire* would be zis! Zee man comes home from zee office, opens zee front door, sees another man's shoes in zee front hall, slowly walks up zee stairs, opens zee bedroom door, sees his wife in bed with another man, waves his hand and calmly exclaims, 'Proceed, sil vous plait!' Zat man – if he proceeds – zat is *savoir faire*!"

CHAPTER TWO

INGENUITY

A Mind Is A Terrible Thing To Taste.

21. CUTTING EDGE TECHNOLOGY.

Four stock brokers are out in the golf course. Standing there on the first fairway, Max is talking into his wristwatch. His friend, Izzy, strolls up to him and says, "Max, what on earth are you doing?"

"What does it looks like I'm doing, Izzy? I'm talking. I'm talking to a client!"

"That's amazing, Max! Your watch is a cell phone?"

"Yes, of course, Izzy, it's the latest thing. I'm too busy to worry about carrying cell phones around. My watch is the very latest in cell phone technology. I can speak into it and hear from it. It's a fabulous time-saver."

On the third hole, Izzy sees Max walking down the fairway, staring into space. He's looking at the sky, but it seems like he's reading something through his glasses. "Max, what are you doing now?"

"I'm reading my email, Izzy."

"Your email, Max? You can read email through your eyeglasses?"

"Yes, Izzy, it's the very latest. I've had a Wi-Fi chip imbedded in my brain and it receives internet messages direct from a satellite and transmits them into my eyeglasses, so that I can scroll through all of my email without even blinking."

"That's fantastic, Max. Now I've heard of everything," gasps Izzy.

On the eighth hole, they arrive at the green and suddenly Izzy notices that Max is nowhere to be found, entirely disappeared. Izzy starts snooping around the shrubbery behind the eighth green, wondering what has happened to his partner. Suddenly, from a bush on the other side of the green, he hears a sound: "Uuuhhhhhhh!" He creeps a little closer to the source of the sound.

"Uuuhhhhhhh!" he hears again. Parting the bushes, Izzy is astonished to see Max squatting on the ground with his trousers halfway down.

"Max! What on earth?"

"Shhhhhh! I'm receiving a fax."

22. THE GROCERY LIST.

A woman is seen in the aisles of a supermarket, going through some strange contortions. As she pushes her cart down the aisle, she's touching her head and her ears with both hands, then her breasts, then her navel, and finally her crotch.

A few minutes later, she is accosted by the store manager. "Madame, I understand you've been walking around my store, making lewd gestures."

"My heavens no," exclaims the woman. "Those aren't lewd gestures. That's my grocery list!"

"Your grocery list? What kind of a grocery list?"

"It's simple word association, sir. It's how I can remember what to buy. First, a head of lettuce," she says, as she's pointing to her skull. "Two ears of corn," she says, grabbing her ears. "Two chicken breasts," she says as she grasps her bosoms. "A half-dozen navel oranges," as she points to her middle. "And Fantastik."

23. ART APPRECIATION.

A group of seven middle-aged ladies are touring the Metropolitan Museum of Art in New York City. During the tour, they are stopped in their tracks by an astounding oil painting, seven feet by four, depicting three grown men, each of them coal black. Against a black background. The only sign of color is a pink penis protruding from the pants of the gentleman in the center of the trio.

The awestruck women are musing for over 20 minutes on the significance of the painting. What was the artist trying to say? They speculate that perhaps it symbolized the dark, ghostly nature of mankind. They speculated that perhaps the artist was trying to symbolize society's emasculation of the black working class.

Their interpretations go on and on.

Suddenly, from across the room strolled an elderly gentleman who addressed the entire group: "Ladies, perhaps I could be of service. I'm the artist of that painting and I saw that you've been admiring it with some puzzlement. In reality, its subject isn't very difficult to interpret."

"Oh, please tell us!" the ladies say, almost in unison.

"Well, actually," said the artist, "it depicts three Scottish coal miners, and the center one went home for lunch."

24. SEMIFORAGING.

A major U.S. Navy aircraft carrier is returning from duty in the Persian Gulf. As it enters the dock area near San Diego, a solitary seaman is seen standing on the tip of the foredeck. He is very excited – he hasn't been home in over a year. As the ship approaches the dock, the captain on the bridge is perplexed to see the seaman begin to send semaphore signals with a set of flags.

His curiosity aroused, the captain keeps his field glasses trained on the young seaman. He sees quite readily that the codes being transmitted are the letters "FF". He then swings his field glasses to the dock and sees a beautiful young woman excitedly jumping up and down, rapidly gesticulating with her own set of semaphore flags. He notes that the message she is sending to her partner on-deck are the letters "EF".

"Ensign! See that seaman up on the foredeck with the semaphore flags? Get him up here on the double. I wanna' know what's going on," barks the captain. Within a couple of minutes, the young seaman is ushered up upon the bridge and has an audience with the captain, his first ever.

"At ease, son, "says the captain. "Now, let's have a little talk together. Something's very fishy going on. You've been sending signals to that woman on the dock. What's happening?"

"Well, sir," says the trembling seaman, "that's my wife down there on the dock. And we were only married six months before I was shipped out. Now I'm about to see her as soon as we tie up and I'm very excited because I haven't seen her in a year."

"And so?" says the captain.

"Well, you see, sir, she is saying that she'd like to eat first."

25.   THE FINAL FINAL EXAM.

Six male seniors from the University of North Carolina are on a lark. They're off to see their brethren at U.V.A. and have a weekend of total abandon and debauchery. However, the inebriation is so total that on Sunday night, they are virtually dead to the world and sleep right on through Monday morning, when they were scheduled to drive back together to school for final exams. Four of the young men in the car are especially distraught, because they are all in the same economics class, whose final exam was taking place at 10 a.m. that Monday morning.

Being resourceful types, however, they cook up an ironclad alibi as they motor back toward campus. They conjure up the scenario that the auto had a flat tire on Sunday evening, and lo and behold, the spare tire was also flat. It just so happened that this was a set of rather rare Michelin tires of a particularly odd size that was difficult to locate. They searched all through Monday morning in Virginia among assorted tire distributors before they finally found the right size and had it installed on the car. It was a scenario guaranteed to win sympathy from any hardnosed professor.

That Monday afternoon, the four delinquent students sheepishly entered the office of their economics professor. In great detail and with stories perfectly corroborated amongst the four, they described their travail the night before and the almost futile search that finally resulted in the securing of the correct tire. They apologized profusely for their absence and beseeched the professor to allow them to take the final exam that afternoon.

The old gray-haired professor raised a suspicious eyebrow, but then smiled broadly and nodded that he would be pleased to administer the final exam to the quartet that afternoon, much to the relief of the students. He asked each of them to return in an hour for the test.

When they returned, the professor handed each a blue essay book and placed each student in a separate classroom alone. He told them they would have one hour for the test.

The students, each in his own abandoned classroom, opened the exam books. Each read with dismay the following questions:

Question Number One: For ten points, explain the Keynesian Theory of Economics.
Question Number Two: For ninety points, which tire went flat?

26. THE LIFESAVER.

A ship captain patrolling the upper deck noticed something odd about one of his lifeboats. Ripping off the covering, he discovered to his amazement a very fresh-faced, dazzling young woman huddled at one end of the boat, intent on devouring a pepperoni pizza.

"Excuse me, ma'am," the captain said, "but exactly what the hell are you doing in there?" The young lady was speechless.

The captain repeated his question with greater vigor and determination. This time, the young lady smiled sweetly, but still remained mute.

"Listen, ma'am, unless you come clean and tell me that you're a stowaway, I'm gonna' have you arrested and locked up," says the captain.

Finally, the girl breaks down in tears and explains through her sobs, "I'm terribly sorry, sir, but my boyfriend is one of your sailors and we're in love and have become so inseparable that neither of us can bear to be apart. Therefore, he found me this humble place to stay while we're en route to Europe."

"In other words," says the captain, "he's keeping you in that lifeboat and you're being screwed every night. Right?" The girl just nodded through her tears.

"Well, you sure are," says the captain. "You may be interested to know that this is the Staten Island Ferry."

27. NOT INVENTED HERE.

A man walks into a noted patent attorney's office, sits down and places a paper bag on the desk.

"I'd like you to go through all of the preparations necessary to have this invention patented, please."

"All right," says the attorney, "let me have a look at the product."

The man removes two apples from the paper bag and places them on the desk.

"Is this some kind of a gag?" says the attorney. "These look like two apples."

"Yes, that's what they look like, but I have developed a totally unique hybrid. Like nothing you've ever seen or tasted before. Go ahead. Take a bite."

The attorney picks up one apple and takes a bite.

"My lord!" the attorney exclaims. "This tastes like the finest vanilla!"

"Right. Now give the apple a quarter turn and have another bite."

"Amazing! This tastes like pure raspberry!"

"Correct. Now give it another quarter turn."

"Wow! This tastes like pure mango!"

"Absolutely. Now give it a final quarter turn."

"Amazing! This tastes exactly like pure papaya!"

"Of course. Now try the other apple."

The attorney bites into the second apple.

"Ugghhh! This tastes like shit!"

"Sorry. Give it one more quarter turn."

28. HISTORICAL NOTE.

A small, graying old man is introduced as a guest on the David Letterman Show. "Tell me, sir," says Letterman, "I understand that you are a noted inventor. Is that true?"

"Yes, very true, David. Lots of inventions."

"Well, why don't you tell our viewing audience what was your most famous invention," says Letterman.

"Okay, David. My two partners and I invented the air conditioner."

"You and your partners invented the air conditioner?" asks Letterman.

"Yes, indeed we did, and we sold the entire patent to Sears, Roebuck."

"Well, Mr. Ginsberg," says Letterman, "that's very strange because I don't recall Sears, Roebuck ever marketing a Ginsberg air conditioner."

"No, of course not. Sears, Roebuck would never market a Ginsberg air conditioner. The merchandisers there put the Kenmore label on it. They called it the Kenmore air conditioner."

"You invented the Kenmore air conditioner?" says Letterman.

"Yes, exactly. Me and my two partners."

"And could you kindly tell our viewing audience how you can prove this fact?"

"Yes, of course," says Ginsberg. "All three of our names appear on every Kenmore air conditioner."

"They do? Where?"

"On the front of every Kenmore air conditioner, right above the dial, you'll see Norm…Hi…and Max."

29. THE WORLD'S MOST INCREDIBLE INVENTION.

Three construction workers are sitting around the jobsite at lunchtime. They each open their lunch boxes and begin an animated conversation. The subject of today's discussion is: what is the most outstanding invention ever conceived by mankind?

"In mah opinion, de most fabulous ting evuh invented by mankind was de TeeVee. Just imagine how amazin' it is to tink dat a bunch of people can be sittin' in a room someweah in New York City right now and you can see 'em or hear 'em in a little box on your table just as if they were here sittin' wid you!"

"Yeah," says the second man, "dat's pretty amazin', but ah tink dat de most incredible ting evah created was radaah! Just imagine, with radaah, you look at the screen and see objects comin' at you anyweah in space and see 'em move everyweah dey go. Now dat's real magic!"

"Well, those tings are real great, fellas," says the third man, "but in mah mind, de single greatest achievement of mankind was de invention of de thermos bottle!"

The other two stare at him in disbelief. "What??" they exclaim in unison. "De thermos bottle?"

"Yeah. The thermos bottle. Just tink. In da morning, your wife packs your lunch and fills dat thermos bottle wid coffee so hot dat you could boil an egg in it! At mid-morning, you opens dat bottle and you pours out dat coffee, and it's still piping hot. Then, when you're finished with da coffee, you rinse out dat bottle and you pour in ice cold lemonade! In mid-afternoon, you opens up dat bottle again and pours out dat lemonade, and it is still as icy cold as Alaska in January! Ain't dat incredible?"

"So?" his two companions ask.

"Don't you understand? I mean…how do it know?"

30. A MUTE POINT.

A mute is about to deliver a speech to an academic audience. After his introduction and applause, he approaches the podium accompanied by his translator. He stands behind the lectern, adjusts his tie, smiles and begins his address. His opening gesticulation is to take both hands, place them on his hair and fluttering them down each side of his neck to his shoulders, symbolizing female coiffeur. Standing beside him, his translator immediately enunciates into the microphone, "Ladies…"

The mute then immediately spreads his arms, bends his elbows, raises his fists and bulges his biceps. He then pumps his arms vigorously.

On cue, the translator immediately enunciates, "…and gentlemen…"

Immediately upon following those words, the mute quickly steps to the side of the lectern and with a sly glance to the translator, he lowers his hand to his groin and commences to perform a frenzied, simulated masturbation.

Disconcerted and baffled, the translator turns to his cohort, squints with a furrowed brow and says in a heavy whisper, "What?"

In response, the mute nods his head and simply continues an even more frenzied simulated masturbation.

Within a few seconds of cogitation, the translator's face suddenly brightens, he nods knowingly, and hastens to continue his translation: "…it gives me great pleasure…"

31. SPACED OUT PROPOSALS.

Assembled at an auditorium in Geneva is a major conclave of the world's leading astrophysicists. They are gathered here to hear the presentation of several important papers, prepared by teams of astrophysicists who have been working on ambitious plans for their nations' next generation of space travel.

One of the most important papers was delivered by a team combining top officials at Cal-Tech and Jet Propulsion Laboratories in California. Their leading spokesman steps to the microphone and begins: "My friends and colleagues, we have a plan that we believe will enable a mission team from NASA to place a man on Mars by the year 2020." He then goes on to describe to the group the technology that would permit this achievement.

Another highlight of the conference is the team from the Moscow Polytechnic Academy, whose spokesman steps to the microphone and announces: "Mine comrades in science, I am proud to report to you that our group has devised a plan that we believe will permit the landing of a man on the planet Venus by the year 2025." He then proceeds to explain to the group the technology of the mission.

But what brings down the house is a presentation by the chairman of the Warsaw Institute of Astrophysics. He stepped to the microphone and stated: "My scientific colleagues and ladies and gentlemen, the Warsaw Institute of Astrophysics is proud to announce that we have completed all plans to enable Poland's space administration to land a man on the sun by the year 2030."

As soon as he completes that announcement, a bewildered, highly audible gasp is heard throughout the august audience. Scientists turn to scientists and begin whispering feverishly, waving their hands in the air, as scientists often do. The murmurs throughout the audience quickly grow to a crescendo. Finally, one French astrophysicist in the first row raises his hand and begs to interrupt. "Please forgive me, monsieur. I don't mean to interrupt, but let me pose a critical question that I believe is of great concern to many of us. If you were to try to land a team on the sun, zey would be burnt to a crisp!"

The speaker smiles politely at his questioner, gives a sly wink to his academic comrades and addresses the audience. "We have already addressed that consideration, of course, and I was interrupted before I had the opportunity to outline to you the key factor in our plan. You see …we're planning to land at night."

32. INFANTILE KVETCH.

A year-old baby is sitting in his highchair, eating his baby food.

Suddenly, he takes the jar of baby food, winds up and hurls it at the kitchen wall, against which it smashes with a horrible and messy crash.

Simultaneously, the little fellow screams, "I hate this shit!"

"Herman!" his mother shrieks, staring at him in stunned disbelief. "Herman! Oh my God, you just spoke. You just said a word. In fact, you spoke a whole sentence! That's fantastic! How long have you been able to speak?"

"Oh, I've been able to speak with perfect fluency for several months now, Mother," the child states.

"Well, that's incredible! I mean, that's just incredible, Herman," his mother screams. "Why haven't you told us? Why haven't you said anything before this?"

"Well frankly, Mother, up 'til now everything's been okay."

33. THE COLLATERAL LOAN.

When David Rockefeller is running Chase Manhattan, a commotion erupts one day in the reception room of his penthouse executive office suite. A well-dressed elderly gentleman is pounding on the counter and demanding to see Mr. Rockefeller.

"But sir, you do not have an appointment with Mr. Rockefeller," explains the receptionist.

"But I vant to take out a loan! I must have a loan today!" emphasizes the gentleman, his voice rising to a cackle.

"But sir, we can easily assign you to a lending officer, and I'll call one immediately," says the receptionist sweetly.

"I don't vant a lending officer! This is a special loan and requires a special negotiation, and I can only negotiate with the top! Tell Mr. Rockefeller that I'm Mr. Greenebaum from Brooklyn, and I demand to see him. He won't regret it. This is an amazing opportunity for the Chase!"

After several more minutes of bantering, hollering and threats, the receptionist finally agrees to speak with an assistant vice president who eventually refers the matter to a vice president, then to an executive vice president, and after an hour and twenty minutes, Greenebaum is finally ushered in to see David Rockefeller. The banker arises from his desk chair, extends his hand and says, "Good morning, Mr. Greenebaum. What can I do for you?"

"Vell, Mr. Rockefeller, I'm here to negotiate a loan, and I'm going to extend a very special rate to the Chase."

"What kind of special rate?" asks the banker.

"Mr. Rockefeller, mine wife and I on this very evening are leaving on a two-week cruise, and I'd like to borrow $5,000. I will repay the loan in two weeks, and for that loan I will pay you interest of $20."

Like a steel trap, Rockefeller's mind quickly computes the rate, and he murmurs, "Well, let's see. Twenty dollars interest for two weeks on $5,000 is well in excess of our standard rates of ten percent. The deal sounds interesting, Mr. Greenebaum. But wait! We don't know you from Adam! You just wandered in here off the street. What kind of collateral can you give us for our $5,000?"

"I knew you were going to ask that, Mr. Rockefeller," smiles Greenebaum with a twinkle, "and here's your collateral!" With that statement, he grandly hands Rockefeller a set of car keys.

"What's this?" asks the banker.

"That's your collateral," says Greenebaum. "Those are the keys to my Mercedes 500 SEL parked at your curb. Come here and look!" He ushers the banker over to the window and directs him to peer down to the curb on Maiden Lane where there sits a Mercedes sedan nestled right beneath the mighty Chase Manhattan Plaza.

"Go ahead. Take it, Mr. Rockefeller. Put it in your garage. That's your collateral."

"Okay, the deal sounds interesting. Sign him up," says Mr. Rockefeller.

When Greenebaum returns two weeks later to repay the loan, he demands to see Rockefeller again. The banker squints at his new borrower with a grimace. "Mr. Greenebaum, we're accepting your loan repayment...but you should be ashamed of yourself!"

"But why, Mr. Rockefeller?"

"Because we've checked you out, Mr. Greenebaum, in the last two weeks. We have your entire profile, and you should be ashamed of yourself. You are a multimillionaire building contractor from Brooklyn with homes in Miami, Palm Springs and East Hampton. Why on Earth would you want to come to us to borrow $5,000?"

Greenebaum hunches over sheepishly and peers up at his lender. "Vell, Mr. Rockefeller, okay, okay, you found me out, and I am ashamed of myself. But, Mr. Rockefeller, I ask you, where else? Where else, for $20 for two weeks, could I park my car in Manhattan?"

34. THE REFUGE.

On the outskirts of Monte Casino, there lived a rather elderly Italian gentleman in a modest home. One day, during confessional at his local church, he blurted out a story to his priest that had never been uttered before. "Father, I must tell you this. Long ago, during World War II, a beautiful woman knocked on the door of my home and asked me to give her refuge from the enemy. I took pity on her and I hid her in my attic."

The priest said to him, "My son, I think that was a wonderful thing that you did and you have absolutely no need to confess that."

But the earnest gentleman went on. "It's worse than that, Father. You see, the young woman started to repay me with sexual favors."

The priest was still unperturbed. "My son, by giving her refuge, you were both in grave danger. Two people who meet under those circumstances can be very tempted to offer bodily comfort to each other. I understand completely. And if you are truly sorry for your actions, you are indeed forgiven."

"Oh, thank you, Father," exclaims the gentleman. "You've taken a tremendous burden of guilt off of my heart. But I do have one more question."

"And what is that?" asks the priest.

"Do you think I should tell her that the war is over?"

CHAPTER THREE

GLOBE TROTTING

Give Us Another Rendition.

35. GENDER ANALYSIS.

We're in Kuwait City, not long after the first Gulf War. Barbara Walters is interviewing a high-ranking Arab sheik. The cameras are rolling.

"You know, Ali," Ms. Walters begins, "I've noticed a very interesting phenomenon since my last visit here. When I was in Kuwait long before the war, I was appalled to find that women had virtually no status. They were not found in the government, in education, in business or any other endeavor. They were kept strictly in the background. In fact, I distinctly remember being here in Kuwait City and watching Arab husbands walking down the street, with their wives trailing 20 paces behind.

"Today, however," says Walters, "the situation is so strikingly different. It appears that women have been truly emancipated, and for that, I compliment you wholeheartedly. Today in Kuwait, I see women in government posts, in high-ranking positions in your corporations, and in major positions in the educational system. Moreover, strangely enough, I look at the average street downtown here in Kuwait City and am amazed to see women walking 20 paces ahead of their husbands. That is truly a remarkable transformation, Ali. How come?"

The sheik smiles and replies: "Land mines."

36. CURIOUS CUSTOMS.

An elderly immigrant appears at the customs office at Ben Gurion Airport in Israel. He is carrying two tattered suitcases. On high security alert as always, the customs officer asks him to please open the first suitcase. He does so. The suitcase is filled with euros. On top of the currency is a large lethal knife. The customs officer looks up at the old man and says, "Would you mind explaining this?"

"Of course," says the old man. "Of course I will explain. For the past 50 years, I have been a dedicated fundraiser for Israel. In this suitcase there are over one million euros. It was my intention to bring these to Israel, to immigrate here and to turn every one of these over to your government as my gift to you and to this wonderful country. If you will escort me to the nearest government office, I will be pleased to present this gift in person."

"That's incredible," says the customs officer, shaking his head in disbelief. "I've never come across this one before in all my years as a customs officer. That's a wonderful gesture that you're making, sir. But now tell me, what is this knife laying on top of the currency?"

"Well, you see, that's how I raised the money. For the past 50 years, my fundraising has consisted of a very simple strategy. I combed the major cities of Eastern and Central Europe. In each one, I would go into the public lounges, enter the men's room, confront the occupant in each stall, and say to him, 'I'm a fundraiser, and if you don't give me ten euros for Israel I will cut your balls off."

"Well, that knife must've been a very convincing instrument for fundraising," the customs officer says. "In fact, that's the most amazing fundraising scheme I've ever heard of! But tell me, sir, what's in the second suitcase?"

The old man hesitates for a moment and then says, "Well, you see, not everyone likes to give money to Israel."

37. OAT CUISINE.

Two elderly, proper and prim English women are touring Spain by motorcar. They are adventuresome souls and made no advance reservations. They happen upon a quaint, tiny Spanish village that boasts a small, quaint bull ring, a small, quaint church and a small, quaint inn. They fall in love with the entire scene and jointly decide to check in.

Once they are properly ensconced in their rooms at the inn, they go down to its diminutive dining room for dinner. It appears to have fine tablecloth service and apparently makes a genuine effort to provide something on the order of world-class dining. The ladies are seated by the head waiter at a table near the window and peer at the menu. Suddenly, one of the ladies spies an elegant platter containing two large spheres. They are covered in a light, luxurious sauce.

"Very interesting and different wouldn't you say?" says the first lady to her partner. The partner nods with enthusiasm. The pair summons the head waiter, and the first lady says, "Tell me, my good man, what's that being served at the next table? It looks quite intriguing."

"Oh, senora, that is one of the specialties of the house – cajones de toro!"

"Oh, my God!" says the first lady. "That sounds truly bizarre! But you know, we're truly intrepid diners and if that's what I think it is, that's somewhat repulsive but we'd still like to try an order, if you please."

"Senora, I'm terribly embarrassed! The truth is that we are a very small, humble village and we only have one bull fight a day. And those were already spoken for this evening. However, if you were to come back tomorrow evening for dinner once again, I think I could save you an order."

Their interest rising to the boiling point, the ladies readily agree and place the assignment with the head waiter.

The next evening, the ladies return to the dining room with even larger appetites and curiosity.

Almost immediately, the head waiter approaches them and says, "Senoras, you are in luck. We have saved an order of cojones for you and you will have these as your entrée this evening! I hope you shall enjoy them."

Sure enough, the entrée is served, the ladies divide the portion and dine with gusto.

When the pair is having coffee, the head waiter approaches again and says, "Senoras, I sincerely hope you enjoyed our specialty."

"Oh my, yes, we did," says the first lady. "They were marvelous. But now that you ask, let me ask one question. We don't want to appear in the least ungrateful, but the two spheres that you served us tonight were considerably smaller than the two large spheres that you served to that next table last evening. Why the difference?"

"Well, senoras," says the maitre d', shrugging his shoulders and smiling weakly, "I'm terribly sorry and I apologize. But you see, some days the bull wins."

38. MEMORABLE MEMENTO.

After 25 years serving the congregation, Rabbi Horowitz is sent on an all-expense trip to the Hyatt Hotel in Maui. Fortunately for the congregation's budget, the rabbi is single and therefore needs only one plane ticket and a single room.

The bellman brings his luggage to the room, shows him a very lovely chamber, accepts the tip and leaves. The rabbi looks around the room and is immediately impressed. There on the dresser rests an iced bottle of Cristal champagne with a card that reads, "IN APPRECIATION OF 25 YEARS OF SELFLESS DEVOTION TO YOUR FLOCK, SIGNED YOUR CONGREGATION."

Then he looks over at the desk and there is a magnificent arrangement of Hawaiian flora and a card that reads, "CONGRATULATIONS, RABBI HOROWITZ, YOUR ENTIRE CONGREGATION WILL BE FOREVER IN YOUR DEBT FOR YOUR QUARTER CENTURY OF DEVOTED SERVICE."

The rabbi is visibly moved by both of these warm gestures. As he regains his composure, he hears a knock on the door. He goes to the door, opens it to find a six-foot lanky, chesty redhead scantily dressed. She says, "Good afternoon, Rabbi. I'm the bonus from your congregation." Rabbi Horowitz looks at her, hesitates, turns immediately about-face and walks over to the desk, where he picks up the telephone, leaving his comely guest standing in the doorway. He dials quickly, and when a voice answers, he screams, "Max! What on Earth have you done? This is the most lascivious, disgusting stunt that I've ever heard of, and I want the names of everyone on your committee who was behind this outrageous caper!" He slams down the phone. Meanwhile, the young lady has turned on her heel and is about to walk down the hallway.

"Hey! Where are you going?"

"Well, you're obviously very mad," says the young lady.

The rabbi dashes out waving his hands. "Wait a minute! Wait a minute! I'm not mad at YOU!"

39. THE DESPERADO.

A cruise liner in the South Pacific is passing what appears to be a deserted island. It contains nothing but a few palm trees and a few rocks and a deserted beach. Suddenly, the first officer on the bridge gasps as he peers through his binoculars. "Captain! Captain! This is amazing. Have a look at this." What he views through the binoculars is a fat, middle-aged, suntanned man in bathing trunks who is standing there on the beach, wildly jumping up and down and waving his arms hysterically.

The captain takes the binoculars from the first officer and has a look. "Oh, yes," says the captain, "yes, every time we pass that island, that same guy is there, going crazy."

40. THE LETDOWN.

It's the week before Christmas and all through the airliner, numerous creatures are stirring until the captain of the El Al plane announces on the loudspeaker. "Ladies and gentlemen, we're now approaching Ben Gurion Airport and are beginning our descent. Please turn off all cell phones, fasten all seatbelts and make sure that your seat backs are in the erect position. Thank you." A few minutes later, the captain speaks again: "Ladies and gentlemen, we're now on the final approach to Ben Gurion Airport, and before we touch down, I'd like to express to all of you who are visiting the Holy Land for the first time a very Merry Christmas…and for those of you who are standing in the aisles, speaking on your cell phones, I'd like to wish you Happy Chanukah and welcome home."

41. SINISTER SERENDIPITY.

A young man is walking down a dark alley deep in the center of Belfast, Northern Ireland. Suddenly, out of the shadows, steps a gunman waving a .45 caliber pistol. "Quick!" whispers the gunman, "which are you – Catholic or Protestant?"

The young man stands there paralyzed, trembling. "Whatever I answer," he thinks to himself, "I have a 50 percent chance of dying."

The young man begins to perspire heavily. "J-Jewish!" he finally answers.

"God is great!" the gunman exclaims. "I must be the luckiest Arab in Belfast!"

42. MYSTERIES OF THE DEEP.

Futterman takes his wife on a cruise to Tahiti for their 50th wedding anniversary. All is going well, but suddenly a freakish storm strikes the cruise ship just as it is nearing Papeete Harbor. Unfortunately, Mrs. Futterman is washed overboard and lost. Grief-stricken, Futterman lands at Papeete, fills out the necessary papers and then flies home. Before he departs, he receives an assurance from the Papeete harbor master that everything possible will be done in an attempt to retrieve his wife's body.

Ten days later, back at his New York office, Futterman receives a cablegram from the harbor master in Papeete. It reads:

"MR. FUTTERMAN:
DIVERS HAVE LOCATED YOUR WIFE'S BODY. DURING AUTOPSY EXAMINATION AUTHORITIES DISCOVERED 30 MILLIMETER PEARL LODGED IN WIFE'S VAGINA. CURRENT APPRAISED MARKET VALUE IS $10,000. PLEASE SEND INSTRUCTIONS. SIGNED: JACQUES MINOT, HARBOR MASTER, PAPEETE."

Futterman issues an immediate reply by cablegram:

"MONSIEUR MINOT:
PLEASE SEND PEARL. RESET TRAP."
FUTTERMAN

43. LADY FARE.

A young, beautiful and entirely nude woman dashes out of the plaza entrance of Chicago's John Hancock office building, races across the pavement to the taxi stand on Chestnut Street, leaps into the cab and screams at the driver, "Get me to O'Hare Airport fast! Step on it!"

The driver reflexively throws the cab into gear, wheels it onto Michigan Avenue and screeches away. Thirty second later, however, he suddenly jams on his brakes, pulls to the curb, and with a stupefied countenance, turns around to confront his passenger.

"Wait a minute, lady! Wait a minute! Hold everything! I must be crazy. How can I take you to O'Hare? You're stark naked! What the hell do you intend to pay me with?"

Instantly the young thing leans back in her seat, spreads her comely thighs, points decisively and exclaims, "With this!" The cabbie immediately throws up his hands with a grimace and opines, "Gee, lady, ain't you got anything smaller?"

44. THE OASIS.

A man is staggering through the desert, dying of thirst.

His bleary, wind-burned eyes keep searching the horizon for the possible sign of an oasis.

Suddenly, as he emerges over a sand dune, lo and behold there before him is a jacket stand. There on display is a rack of sport coats of every description. The proprietor greets him with open arms and a huge smile.

"Oh boy, is this your lucky day! Almost everything is on sale!"

"Water…water!" murmurs the man as he drops to his knees. "Just give me water."

"I'm sorry. We have no water here," says the proprietor, "but we have fantastic bargains on navy blue blazers, or how about a marvelous Harris tweed? I have one in just your size. Or how about this beautiful two-button camel's hair model, or this fabulous charcoal gray cashmere number? They're all on sale! Take your pick!"

"Water…water!" yells the man, crawling toward the racks of merchandise. "Just give me water."

"Gee, I'm really sorry that we don't have any water, but I can offer you this fantastic muted hounds tooth three-button number – very British – with a belt in the back. Looks like just your style. How about it?"

The man just staggers to his feet and shakes his head, continuing his dejected journey across the burning sands. A few more miles and he mounts another sand dune to behold yet another retailing extravaganza. This time, it's a tie stand, racks and racks of ties of every description. The proprietor is standing there grinning from ear-to-ear, ready to make a sale. "Hello, there! Have you ever come to the right place! Believe it or not, every tie you see here is on sale today, and I mean deep discounts."

"Water…water," croaks the man.

"Gee, I'm terribly sorry, but we don't have a drop of water on the premises, but I can offer you these all-silk reps and paisleys at 50 percent off. Or how about these very chic, small-patterned numbers in every shade of blue and in every shade of red! Or how about these fabulous bowties! Or we even have a wonderful Western cowboy string tie, if that's your style!"

The man just shakes his head wearily and mutters, "Water...I've just got to have water," and staggers on across the burning sands.

A few miles later, he is just about to expire when all of a sudden he sees in the distance an oasis, a true oasis. Wait, is it a mirage? He crawls closer and closer on his hands and knees. No, it's not a mirage. It's a real oasis! There it is, a green splendor of lush palm trees waving in the breeze and sparkling fountains spurting silvery streams of water high into the air! He crawls faster and faster. Finally, he is at the main gate which is manned by a uniformed, armed sentry. He attempts to crawl past the sentry, but his path is blocked.

"I'm sorry, sir, but you cannot be admitted."

"Oh, my God. Why?"

"Jackets and ties are required."

45. KIBBITZING KIBBUTZIM

A large Texas oilman is touring Israel. When he visits a kibbutz in the Northern Galilee, he is escorted for the day's excursion around the property by an elderly, bearded, wizened kibbutzim.

As they travel by jeep around the fields, where inhospitable terrain had been transformed into lush, green, fertile land, the Texas is obviously impressed. Nevertheless, halfway through the tour, he says to his elderly companion, "You know, mah friend, y'all have done a very creditable job with this property, and Ah see that you really have extensive acreage. But you might be interested to know that mah ranch in Texas is so big that you can start driving at dawn in one direction and by sunset, you haven't reached the end of mah property."

The aging tour guide nods pensively and says, "Yes, yes, I remember …I used to have a car like that."

CHAPTER FOUR

THE ANIMAL KINGDOM

Robbing P.E.T.A. To Pay Paul

46. THE ARTICULATE CANINE.

A man is walking past a modest home, when he does a double-take. He sees a sign in the window that says simply: TALKING DOG FOR SALE.

Burning with curiosity, he knocks on the door. When the home owner opens it, he says, "Do you really have a talking dog for sale?" The man replies in the affirmative.

"You mean he talks? You mean you have a dog that really can talk?" Again, the homeowner nods. "May I see him?"

"Of course. He's out back. You're welcome to go have a conversation."

The visitor is now dazzled and can't wait to exit the rear door and finds, sitting lazily in the sunshine on the backyard grass, a small, unassuming schnauzer. Timidly, the visitor approaches the dog and sits on the grass beside him. "Do you talk?"

"Yes, I talk," says the schnauzer.

The visitor sits there, stupefied. When he can finally collect his thoughts and ask another question, he says, "How long have you talked? How long have you been able to speak English?"

"Most of my life," says the schnauzer. "It just came very naturally, since I've always been around people."

"But, but what kind of life have you led?" asks the visitor breathlessly. "This is all so incredible!"

"Well, if you must know," says the dog, "when they found out I could talk, they immediately recruited me for the CIA. I was, of course, assigned to the covert division and went through extensive training in espionage. Once that was over, they assigned me to various foreign capitals at which they could smuggle me into the boardrooms of many heads of state in important nations. My assignment was to sit there unobtrusively beneath the table, listen to the proceedings and deliberations, and then faithfully report back to my handlers."

"Astounding!" says the visitor.

"After an extensive career performing gallantly for my country, I retired from the CIA and entered the field of industrial espionage. It was a natural career extension for me. My clients would smuggle me into the boardrooms of major corporations throughout the world, and I would be assigned to sit there beneath the table, listen to the deliberations, and report back to my handlers. I learned innumerable trade secrets, of course, and was able to transmit these to my clientele."

"Dumbfounding!" says the visitor.

"At that point, I had earned enough to retire, I found a very lovely mate, settled down and had puppies. Today, this home provides just the kind of retirement atmosphere that suits me."

With that, the visitor leaps to his feet, dashes back through the rear door of the home and says to the owner, "How much do you want for that dog?"

"Seventy-five bucks," says the owner.

The visitor is stupefied. "Seventy-five bucks! Seventy-five bucks! That's outlandish! That dog really can talk. Why on Earth are you asking only $75?"

"Because he's such a fucking psychopathic liar!"

47. LONG DISTANCE LOVER.

It is almost twilight in the Masai Mara of Kenya. A group on safari is stunned and saddened to see a mouse laying in the middle of the savanna grass, gasping for breath. The group is very distressed to see this trauma and immediately begins to administer CPR to the mouse. Within a few minutes, the mouse regains full consciousness and is able to speak. "What happened? What happened?"

"Are you able to breathe? You look almost dead from exhaustion!"

"Oh boy! Wow!" says the mouse, continuing to gasp as he tries hard to regain his breathing capacity. "I've had an absolute killer experience!"

"What happened to you?"

"Well, I was walking through the grassland this morning as usual, and I spied this giraffe. She was a fantastic giraffe. She was the most gorgeous giraffe I had ever seen. I fell in love instantly. She responded very readily. We made fantastic love all day long. And between the kissing and the fucking, I must've run 500 miles!"

48. REINCARNATION BOUQUET.

Cinderella's luck has run out. She is sitting at home, alone and destitute. Her handsome prince died years ago, leaving her heavily in debt. She even had to hock her glass slippers. The only possession she still has left is a tattered old tomcat, left over from the former days. Now she just sits in her solitary confinement, reflecting on her former life of grandeur, despondent with her fate.

Suddenly she arises, stares out the window and exclaims, "Fairy Godmother, Fairy Godmother, where are you when I need you most? You were there for me when I was mistreated by my wicked stepsisters, and you were there for me when I needed glass slippers and a pumpkin chariot and a prince. But what good is all that now? Where are you when I really need you the most?"

Suddenly there is a puff of smoke and standing there before her, in her humble living room, is none other than the original Fairy Godmother.

"For Christ's sake, Cinderella, quit your crying. How many times do I hafta' help you?"

"But I really need you now, Fairy Godmother, more than ever! My creditors are beating my door down, I'm about to be taken to the poorhouse and I'm old and wrinkled and gray, and I would only love to have my youth back."

"Okay, no problem. I'm gonna' give you the business one last time. I'm gonna' come through for you." With that, the Fairy Godmother waves the wand and poof, Cinderella finds herself in a lavish penthouse apartment, surrounded by an array of corporate bond coupons and healthy bankbooks. She looks in the mirror and discovers, to her delight, that all of the wrinkles have fled and she is young and beautiful once again. She is overjoyed.

"But wait, Fairy Godmother! What good is all this if I can't have my prince back?"

"Boy, you really want everything, don't you? Okay, you horny bitch, you can have your goddamn prince back, too. Here he is." She waves the wand again and turns the cat into the handsome prince.

The background music swells, she and her prince embrace. They are reunited, and as he holds her in his arms, he gently whispers in her ear, "Now aren't you sorry you had me neutered?"

49. THE HANDICAPPER.

It is another race day and crowds have assembled for the sport of kings. New York's Belmont Raceway is buzzing with excitement.

A veteran devotee of the sport decides to nose around the paddock a bit before betting on the first race. As he saunters among the stalls, he is intrigued to see a rabbi standing with both hands placed over the forehead of one nag, muttering phrases in Hebrew. The racing fan thought this was rather peculiar and decides to jot down the name and number of the horse. Within a few minutes, he watches as the trainer leads the horse out of the paddock and toward the track.

Lo and behold, the race fan watches that very horse win the first race by four lengths! Mentally, he kicks himself for failing to follow an instinct and place a bet on that horse. Immediately, he arises from his seat, walks downstairs and back to the paddock, where he is now thunderstruck to see the same rabbi at a different stall, with both hands over the forehead of a different horse, once again muttering in Hebrew. And again, the trainer later appears, leads the horse out to the track, and the horse becomes a starter in the second race.

The race fan is increasingly intrigued, but has already gone to great lengths to study the racing forms and has several bets down on competing horses in the second race.

Lo and behold, the horse that the rabbi had just addressed goes on to win the second race by ten lengths!

Now, the race fan is truly agitated. He heads for the paddock on the double, and sure enough, there's the same rabbi at yet another stall, with both hands placed over the forehead of another horse, and again muttering lowly in Hebrew. The race fan doesn't even wait for the trainer to appear. He dashes to the betting windows and places a $10,000 bet on the nose of this nag. The third race is now about to begin and there is his newly blessed nag in the starting gate. The bell rings. They're off! His blessed horse in the third race takes about four strides out of the starting gate and collapses dead on the track. The race fan's eyes grow as big as saucers; he almost collapses in a fit of hysteria upon witnessing this disaster. As the track attendants come out to drag his horse's carcass off the track and very likely prepare to send it to the glue factory, he springs back down to the paddock. There he encounters the very same rabbi.

He dashes up to the rabbi and screams, "Rabbi! What happened? What happened? You blessed that horse in the first race and he won by four lengths. You blessed that horse in the second race and he won by ten lengths. You blessed another horse in the third race and he dropped dead right out of the starting gate! How could that be?"

The diminutive rabbi looks at the stranger from under shaggy eyebrows, gives his cigar a few taps, shrugs his shoulders and whispers, "That's the trouble with you Reformed Jews. You don't know the difference between a brucha and a kaddish!"

50. MASS MARKET APPEAL.

In a small Midwestern town is a sign in a shop window. It reads:

JOHN SMITHERS – TAXIDERMIST AND VETERINARIAN. EITHER WAY, YOU GET YOUR CAT BACK.

51. NO BUSINESS LIKE SHOW BUSINESS.

The Bronx Zoo is in dire straits. Budget cuts have forced the purse strings to become tighter and tighter. Finally, a crisis looms when one of its main attractions, a big male gorilla, passes away. Finding it impossible to send a safari to Africa to obtain a new gorilla, or even buy a used gorilla on the open market from another zoo, the director of the Bronx Zoo resorts to tactics that would otherwise be far beneath him. He places an ad in *The New York Post* classified section and also on-line. It says, "PROMINENT NEW YORK CITY INSTITUTION SEEKS EXPERIENCED ACTOR WILLING TO IMPERSONATE AN ANIMAL."

The next day, Sheldon Rabinowitz, an out-of-work Broadway actor, down on his luck, applies for the job. He sits there in the director's office and listens to an astounding assignment. He is briefed on the budget cuts and all of the desperate tactics to which the zoo must now resort. His assignment is to don a gorilla costume and impersonate a live gorilla in the gorilla cage for the benefit of New York's zoo patrons.

Sheldon considers the assignment to be a humiliating prospect, but nevertheless accepts the challenge because he needs the money. The next day, he reports for duty, conscientiously dons the gorilla attire, steps into the cage and begins to perform his antics. When old ladies and children appear, he delights them by jumping up and down and screeching and scratching his armpits. Sheldon swings from tires and climbs up fake branches of the fake trees in his cage and truly puts on a rather marvelous show for the public. But on the third day, he's violently swinging on his tire when it swoops him into the next cage, and to his shock, he lands roughly at the bottom of the lion cage. Frozen with fear, he gazes at the lion as it approaches him, licking his chops. Sheldon is backed against the bars by the lion and as he sees his life pass before his eyes, he suddenly hears, to his astonishment, from the lion, the words, "Yiskadal…"

And almost immediately, he hears a heavy, angry whisper from the third cage, coming from a giant panda, saying, "Shut up, you schmucks, or you'll get us all fired!"

52. INSEMINATION NATION.

It is evening at a country tavern on the outskirts of Topeka. A chicken farmer is sitting alone in the bar, caught up in high elation and toasting all those cohorts around him. Then, an attractive, very pregnant young woman enters the tavern and sits down on the stool next to his. He immediately orders some champagne for her.

"Many thanks, my friend," she says, "but what's the big celebration?"

"Well, ma'am, I'm celebrating the fact that I've overcome an immense problem in my henhouse. It seems that I encountered an incredible streak of infertility and I was going broke because my hens simply were not laying eggs."

The young lady sipped her champagne and raised an eyebrow. "That's interesting," she says. "I had the same problem for two years in trying to have a baby. Isn't that a coincidence? And exactly how did you manage to solve the problem?"

"I switched cocks," explained the farmer.

"What a coincidence," said the lady.

READ AT YOUR OWN RISQUE!

53.   THIEF OF BAGHDAD REPRISE.

On the streets of Baghdad, a thief is apprehended by the police and charged with the theft of a pocketful of pomegranate seeds.

When Saddam Hussein happens to hear about the incident, he decides on a whim to give his court some amusement and commands that the culprit be brought before him. When the virile young captive is ushered into the great chamber and brought before Hussein, the sadistic ruler informs him of his fate: "Young man, the crime you have committed is punishable by death; however, for our amusement, we shall give you an opportunity to save your miserable hide. You shall have to successfully pass three tests, and if you can achieve this, we shall spare your life. In the lower level of this palace are three rooms. In the first room, you will find a jug containing three gallons of Iraqi wine. If you are able to consume all three gallons in the space of an hour, you shall have successfully passed the first test. We shall then usher you into the second room, in which there is a fierce female Bengal tiger with an abscessed tooth. If you are able to successfully extract that tooth with your bare hands, you will have passed the second test. In the third chamber is a 19-year-old Iraqi maiden. She is a lovely virgin. In the space of an hour, if you are able to entirely satisfy that maiden and she signs an affidavit to that effect, then you shall have passed the third test and your life shall be spared. Are you ready?"

The young man winces, shrugs his shoulders and says, "Well, I guess I don't have a lot to lose. Show me the room with the wine."

Two burly guards usher the young man into a lower chamber while Hussein and his court buzzes with anticipation outside the chamber.

In just less than an hour, the young man knocks on the door, asking to be released, and in a drunken stupor staggers out into the hallway, pointing to an empty jug on the floor. He is greeted by applause from his audience. "Okay," he says, slurring his words, "show me that room with that Bengal tiger!" The guards immediately steer him into the next chamber from which resounding growls and roars can be heard. The Bengal tigress is in obvious pain.

Once the door is closed with the young man locked inside, there ensues 20 minutes of furious commotion. The ruler and his court stand by outside in rapt silence. Finally comes the knock for release. The guards throw open the chamber door and there, in everyone's view, is the tigress at the far end of the chamber, laying on the floor on her back, exhausted. Staggering toward the door is the young man, covered from head to foot with blood and lacerations. He is panting furiously. "Okay …okay…now show me that room with the maiden with the abscessed tooth!"

54. THE CRASS MENAGERIE.

Max and Seymour are two New York senior citizens living on the Upper West Side. They are sitting on a bench on a little grassy plot on Upper Broadway, watching the world go by.

"Look what's happened to this neighborhood, Max," laments Seymour. "Oy vay, is it going to pot. Every vierdo in the world is valking around here. Just look at this street. Cocaine pushers over there. Crack addicts over here…"

"Oy, Seymour, that's not the half of it. Nowadays, just look at all the sex freaks…all the rapists…the transvestites…and do you know that some of these people are even into bestiality?"

"Vat? Vat's bestiality, Seymour? Vat's dat?"

"You know, Max. That's when people are copulating with goats… with pigs…with sheep…with chickens…"

"Chickens? Feh!"

55.   VULTURE VENTURE.

The farmer has a serious problem. Egg production in his henhouse has fallen off 50 percent. Drastic measures are necessary. He drives into town to see a solution. It seems that he has heard tales about a legendary Super Rooster, one with prodigious impregnation capacities.

He finds the dealer and inquires about this legendary creature. "Well, you've come to the right place, sir. I, indeed, have a Super Rooster, and he is available for sale."

"How much?"

"For you today a special deal – only $5,000."

"Five thousand dollars? That's an incredible price!"

"Yes, but he has incredible capacities. He will solve your total egg production problem."

The farmer relents, pays the ransom and drives home with his Super Rooster. He immediately lets the rooster loose in the henhouse and hopes for the best.

Sure enough his investment pays off handsomely. Before long the hens are all clucking merrily in a paroxym of satisfaction, and eggs are being produced at a record rate. Elated with his ROI, the farmer basks in the glory of his wisdom.

Then one day, to his shock and horror, the farmer finds the Super Rooster missing. The little bird is nowhere to be found. He searches the henhouse in vain, he searches the grounds – all to no avail. Suddenly, as he peers out across one of his bare, newly planted fields, he sees a large vulture slowly circling its prey. The farmer begins to walk toward that spot. He keeps his eye on the fluttering vulture as it swoops in lazy circles lower and lower. As he approaches the scene, the farmer spots a tiny creature on the ground immediately below the vulture's concentric circles. The farmer breaks into a dead run. Could it be? He runs faster, in a panic. Yes! There on the ground, laying on its back, is the Super Rooster! Its little claws are pointed straight up in the air, its forlorn little head is against the ground, its tiny beak pointing straight up.

"Oh, my lord!" cries the farmer. "It's my rooster. He totally expired from exhaustion. He had given his all for me. He gave his last effort for my cause! The poor little bird! Well, the least I can do is give him a decent burial and keep him from being torn to bits by that wretched vulture!"

The farmer rushes up to the spot where the rooster's body lies motionless as the vulture swoops even lower. The farmer kneels and is about to cradle the poor little hero's body in his arms and cart him off to a decent burial. He bends lower. Suddenly, the rooster opens one eye and says, "Pssssssssst! Get away! Get away!"

The farmer is totally dismayed. "You're alive! Thank God! What's going on?"

The rooster whispers again in growing irritation, "Get away! Get away! If you want to fuck with vultures, you have to play their silly games!"

56. PUTTING ON THE DOG.

Lyman and Hyman are walking their dogs down Park Avenue. Lyman has a Great Dane and Hyman has a Chihuahua. After a few blocks, they acquire a thirst and mutually decide to head for a side street bar. After selecting the oasis of their choice, Lyman walks in first with his Great Dane.

Instantly, the bartender screams, "Hey, you! Get that fucking dog out of here. You know that dogs aren't allowed in this bar!" Lyman turns to leave when Hyman enters with his Chihuahua on a leash.

Once again the bartender screams, even louder, "Hey, you! Get that fucking dog out of here! You know dogs aren't allowed in this bar!"

Hyman stands there and looks at the bartender with a blank stare. "But, sir, you don't understand. I'm blind, and this is my seeing-eye dog."

"Are you nuts?" screams the bartender. "That's nothing but a pipsqueak little Chihuahua!"

Hyman looks dismayed and replies, "They gave me a Chihuahua?"

57. BEAR WITH ME.

Jake and Isadore are camping in Yellowstone. It's their first time ever. This morning they are sitting in their pup tent, eating their bowls of Special K when, all of a sudden, Jake cries out in horror, "Izzy, oh my God, look!"

There in the clearly, 40 yards away, stands a gigantic grizzly heading right for the tent.

"Oh, wow!" exclaims Izzy as he begins feverishly to put on his running shoes.

"Izzy, you schmuck! What are you doing that for? Don't you realize that zoologists say that an American grizzly bear can run at twice the speed of a human being?"

"I don't have to outrun the bear, Jake," says Izzy as he laces up and arises. "All I have to do is outrun you."

58. THRILL OF THE HUNT.

A man garbed in a splendid hunting outfit is hiking through the woods in the wilds of Northern Canada, his high-powered rifle at the ready, seeking the famed Canadian grizzly.

He isn't more than an hour away from his hunting lodge when suddenly out of the brush behind him emerges a giant male grizzly bearing a gargantuan erection. The grizzly grabs him from behind, his giant paws encircling the hunter's chest, and his huge jaws hovering right above the hunter's quivering head.

"Oh, my God! Don't kill me! Please don't kill me!" cries the hunter.

"Okay, okay," says the bear. "Drop your pants!"

The hunter instantly obeys the gigantic, hairy being behind him and drops his elegant hunting trousers. In a flash, the bear rams his gigantic member up the rectum of the hapless hunter. When finally satisfied, the bear releases his prey, leaves the hunter in a crumbled, disheveled heap on the ground and trots off into the forest.

The very next day, determined to have revenge, the hunter leaves his hunting lodge, armed with an even more sophisticated rifle, plus a few pieces of electronic detection gear slung around his neck. Once again, he is hardly more than an hour away from the hunting lodge on his woodland trek, and despite exercising the greatest amount of caution, he is once again ambushed from the rear by the very same grizzly. Once again, he panics as he feels those giant paws encircle him and once again he cries out the instinctive plea for mercy. Once again, he hears the familiar command, "Drop your pants," and reluctantly, but obediently, he complies. The bear engages in his customary orgy and again leaves his victim in a crumpled, quivering heap on the ground. In a twinkling, the bear disappears into the brush.

The next day, more determined that ever, the hunter equips himself with the absolute state-of-the-art in detection and high-powered riflery. Off he goes into the same woods to even the score.

This time he uses every human and electronic precaution possible to get a first sight of his prey before being ambushed again. He creeps through the brush like a commando, his head on a virtual swivel.

Alas, it is all to no avail, and before he can even blink, he feels that same sudden attack from the rear, and the giant paws claiming him captive once again. Without even waiting for the familiar command, the hunter automatically drops his pants and awaits the severe penalty.

But before proceeding, this time the bear holds him close, bends over and whispers in his ear, "You know, fella…you're not really into hunting, are you?"

59. PULLING HIS LEG.

A traveling salesman stops by a farm house and, after making his pitch, is invited to have some iced tea on the veranda. As he sits chatting with the farmer, he happens to notice a three-legged pig that is laying at the farmer's feet like a dog.

"It's interesting that you keep a pig around here like a pet," says the salesman.

"Yes," says the farmer, "this is a very interesting pig. In fact, this is a truly heroic pig. Do you know what this pig has done? Three years ago, one of our infants was lost out in the field, and this pig took it upon itself to search around the cornfield until it found our daughter and then squealed loud enough to attract everyone's attention and we located the missing child. Two years ago, I had an accident out on the back 40 acres when my tractor tipped over and pinned me underneath it. That pig sensed my danger and started squealing loud enough for the other farm hands to come and find me and get me released. Otherwise, I could have perished under the weight of that tractor. Then early this year, when our house was being burglarized one night, this pig heard the intruder, attacked him and drove him off the property."

"I'm very impressed," says the salesman. "But tell me. I'm curious to know why that pig only has three legs."

"Well, frankly," says the farmer, "a pig like that you don't eat all at once."

CHAPTER FIVE

FATEFUL ENCOUNTERS

It's Been Nice No-ing You.

60. MYSTERY MAN.

A tall, youthful stranger walks into a rural tavern in the back hill Country of Tennessee.

Not accustomed to seeing strangers in these parts, the young man is eyed suspiciously by the locals as they gulp down their evening moonshine. Finally, one of the locals saunters up to the stranger and says, "Hey, good buddy, how's the evenin'?" The young man smiles and says hello. He notes that the locals around the bar are becoming nervous and fidgety. He senses that strangers don't venture into these quarters very frequently.

The first local eyes him up and down, with his head cocked and finally squints and says, "You ain't from around these parts, are ye?"

"No, I'm really not," says the young man.

On edge over the fact that the young stranger might be a Revenue agent or an ATF man, the group spokesman gets the vibes that his friends have the same apprehensions.

After a few more moments, he asks, "Just how far away are you from, buddy?"

"Actually, I'm a Canadian citizen touring the US," the young man responds.

The local spokesman inquires a little further. "Ah see. And exactly what do you do for a livin' up there?"

"I'm a taxidermist."

The local gets nervous again. "A taxidermist? Exactly what's a taxidermist? That ain't got nothin' to do with collectin' taxes, does it?"

"No, not at all. I mount animals."

Brightening and heaving a sigh, the local spokesman throws his hands up in the air, turns to his friends and says, "Hey, guys, he's one of us!"

61. FEARLESS FORECASTING.

On a large Indian reservation in South Dakota, the tribal chief calls the Black Hills office of the National Weather Service.

"Hello. May I ask a question? Thank you. I know it's only September, but I'm wondering whether you're forecasting winter weather as yet. Oh, yes? You are? Well, please let me have an early forecast. Oh, yes? Pretty cold, huh? Colder than normal, huh? OK, thanks so much." The chief clicks off his cell phone and summons his tribal council from around the entire territory.

When they are all assembled the next evening around his campfire, he speaks to them his words of wisdom. "Guys, the National Weather Service is forecasting a colder winter than normal, and I think it is only prudent that we have our brethren get out there and comb the woods and collect an extra-heavy supply of firewood for this winter." The tribal council nods obediently and the next day sends out the word.

It's now October and the chief starts to worry again. He pulls out his cell phone and once again calls the National Weather Service. "Good morning, I'm inquiring about your current forecast for winter weather. Does it still look like sub-normal temperatures? Oh, yes? And would you say exceptionally cold? That's interesting. Thank you very much."

Once again, the chief summons his tribal council and sends out the word that the winter weather may be exceptionally cold and that everyone should redouble efforts to collect firewood.

Now it's November, and the chief is getting even more nervous. He calls the National Weather Service again. "Good morning, I'm wondering if you've updated your forecast for the winter in South Dakota. You have? You're now predicting extreme cold? Truly bitter cold? Thank you very much."

The chief calls the tribal council again and announces crisis conditions. All available manpower must be pressed into service in collecting firewood throughout the Black Hills, and making sure that the reservation firewood supply is at record levels. A week later, one of the top officials of the National Weather Service, Washington, DC, is visiting his Black Hills branch. In talking with the branch manager, he says, "By the way, John, I'm curious about something. I noticed that each month, your forecast for winter weather in South Dakota has gotten progressively more pessimistic, and that you are now forecasting extreme cold conditions, bordering on new records. Upon what data are you basing this?"

"Sir, it's based on the fact that the fucking Indians are collecting firewood like crazy."

62. GETTING DUCKS IN A ROW.

One rainy evening in Lower Manhattan, a nicely dressed young man walks into a tavern and sits down at a bar, ordering a Martini. A few moments later, he reaches into his raincoat pocket and produces a foot-high little man in white tie and tails and sets the little creature on the bar. He then proceeds to reach into his other pocket and withdraw a miniature grand piano, which he also sets on the bar. Finally, from still another pocket, he produces a tiny piano bench. He sets the bench beside the piano and the miniature musician elegantly takes its seat, pauses to peer around the room at the awestruck patrons, and then proceeds to play the Rachmaninoff Third Piano Concerto.

All occupants of the tavern are stupefied. As the tiny musician completes the piece, they rise as one and give him a thundering ovation. The musician arises, turns and bows graciously.

On the next bar stool has been perched a Yuppified stockbroker who is thoroughly mesmerized by the performance. As the applause subsides, he asks the full-sized gentleman who produced all this, "Where in the world did you find that marvelous miniature musician?"

The mysterious stranger in the raincoat sips his martini and exclaims, "A genie gave him to me. Actually, the genie gave me a magic lamp and told me to rub it and ask for anything I wish!"

"Wow!" said the young stockbroker, "could I possibly see that magic lamp?"

"Of course," says the stranger, as he reaches down and grasps his satchel from the floor, opens it and removes a tiny little brass oil lamp.

"Amazing! I mean, like, how exciting!" gasps the young man. "Do you think I could actually borrow it for a moment and give it one little rub?"

"Sure," says the stranger. "Here, go ahead and give it a rub, but I've got to warn you, this lamp was bestowed by an extremely dyslexic genie…"

The young stockbroker grabs the lamp in a twinkling and begins to rub it gleefully as he exclaims, "Oh, wow! Come on, genie. Let's see a million bucks!"

For a few awkward moments nothing happens. The stockbroker continues to rub the lamp, he looks at the stranger, the stranger looks back at him quizzically and fellow bar patrons gather near in rapt anticipation. There is total silence for more agonizing moments.

Suddenly, the tavern door bursts open and into the tavern flow a flock of ducks. They keep coming and coming and coming. They flood the entire tavern. Their little wings are flapping, and their little bills keep quacking and quacking. They are everywhere. They are filling the room to the brim. They're on top of everybody and everything.

The horrified stockbroker pleads in agonized tones to the stranger, "Wait a minute! Wait a minute! I didn't ask for a million *ducks*!"

"That's right," says the bemused stranger. "And do you think that I asked for a 12-inch pianist?"

63. FORKED TONGUE TALK.

A man sits down next to a beautiful blonde in a bar and after some casual conversation reaches into his pocket and produces a small frog, which he sets up on the bar in front of her.

"Madam, I'll have you know that this is no ordinary frog. This frog happens to have the world's longest tongue and he is trained to perform incredible oral sex upon women."

"Oh, come on," says the blonde, "that's the wildest story I ever heard!"

"Ah, but it's true!" says the gentleman. "Would you like me to prove it to you? He could easily give you a free demonstration!"

"Are you kidding?" says the blonde, her curiosity mounting.

"Not on your life," says the gentleman. "Step with me into the next room, where we can have some privacy, and I'll ask Sylvester to give you a personal demonstration."

Her curiosity now uncontrollable, the blonde arises and follows the gentleman into the billiard parlor, where they close and lock the door.

"Now, madam, if you would be kind enough to remove your clothes and mount that billiard table on your back with your legs spread, I will instruct Sylvester to proceed."

With excitement tempered by lingering skepticism, the blonde demurely disrobes, mounts the billiard table and spreads her legs. The gentleman then carefully places the frog on the green felt squarely between her widespread creamy white thighs.

The little green amphibian crouches there motionless, staring at the vaginal display ahead of him, and then turning his head to look at his master and then back again to stare at the blonde beauty. For many uncomfortable moments he remains motionless. The blonde sighs impatiently. Still nothing. Finally, in exasperation, the gentleman reaches over and removes the frog to the side of the table while exclaiming, "Okay, Sylvester...this is the last time I'm going to show you!"

64. HEADS UP.

A young man enters one of those posh, trendy bars in Beverly Hills and sits himself down on a barstool. He is well-dressed. He is of average height and build. In fact, there is nothing really notable about him at all, except for one aspect – his head is the size of a tennis ball.

The bartender takes note of this fact immediately upon the arrival of his new customer, but tries hard not to reveal his shock at the sight. For the entire first hour that the patron is sitting there, slowly imbibing two frozen drinks, the bartender tries and tries in vain to keep from staring at the freakish anomaly. Finally, the agitated bartender cannot contain his composure a moment longer and, as the crowd begins to thin out, leans across the bar and whispers to the patron, "Sir, would you mind terribly if I ask you a highly embarrassing question?"

"Of course not. Go right ahead."

"Well…sir…I mean, I was wondering about…well, you know…"

The patron jauntily tapes his diminutive noggin and grins. "Oh, you mean this? Of course. And you want to ask me whether it was always this size? Was I born with it this way?"

"Yes, sir, might I ask that?" said the bartender timidly.

"Of course you can! And I'll be delighted to tell you – no, it was not always this size. Up until last year, it was a perfectly normal size, just like yours or anyone else's. But then a funny thing happened. I was in the South Pacific exploring a deserted island. I was walking along the beach when all of a sudden, I discovered an old bottle. I picked it up, examined it, rubbed it and lo and behold, out of the bottle emerged this huge, fantastic genie. It was in the form of a giant, gorgeous, voluptuous woman."

"What happened then?" said the bartender, his eyes widening.

"Well, I just fell to my knees in amazement and looked at her and gasped. She said to me, 'Congratulations! This is thy lucky day. I intend to grant thee one wish immediately. Pray tell me what it shall be?" Well, I exclaimed that she was the most incredibly beautiful woman I had ever seen and my one wish was to have immediate intercourse with her. But also, she replied, 'Oh, you have asked me for the one thing that I cannot give you. Please ask me for anything else.' So I said, 'Okay, how about a little head?'"

65. JOIN THE CLUB.

A tall, lanky used car salesman from Dallas is paying a first-time visit to Greenwich Village. He ambles into a cozy little bar, spies a magnificently preserved blonde on one of the first barstools and suavely plops himself down on the empty stool next to her.

As he promptly proceeds to administer his well-rehearsed pick-up lines in an immediate campaign to win her favors for the evening, the young lady, obviously a denizen of the neighborhood, gives her enthusiastic visitor a withering glance and murmurs softly, "Forget it, honey. You've got the wrong gal."

The perplexed Texan immediately responds, "Excuse me, ma'am, but how come?"

"For the simple reason, fella, that I happen to be a lesbian," she replies.

The perplexed Texan fingers his Budweiser nervously, furrows his brow, cocks his balding head, sports a sheepish grin and says, "Excuse me again, ma'am, but this is mah first time here in town and I guess ah'm just not hip to all the New York lingo. What exactly is a lesbian?"

Rolling her eyeballs until they almost disappear into her sockets, the middle-aged blonde sighs a deep sigh, swings herself around and explains, "Okay, look. Let me put it to you this way, sweetheart. Do you see that incredibly gorgeous redhead down at the other end of the bar? I mean the young one in the ponytail with the huge tits. See her?"

"Yes, ah sure do, ma'am."

"Well, I have a tremendous compulsion right now to walk over there and rip her blouse off and run my mouth entirely over those breasts!"

The Texan sits there staring at the young redhead in the distance, then peers at his drinking partner, then back to the redhead, then back to his drinking partner. "You know something, ma'am?" He finally murmurs, "Ah must a lesbian, too!"

66. AN EDUCATION IN DEFECATION.

It's 2:00 a.m. and not long before closing time at the Oak Bar in New York's Plaza Hotel. A very well-dressed drunk stumbles in and sits down at the end of the bar. He signals the bartender, summoning him for an order and a conversation.

"What is it you'd like to discuss, sir?" says the bartender.

"I'd like to discushhh nuclear physishks."

"All right, sir, I'm at your service. Let's begin discussing nuclear physics."

"Jusht a minute," says the drunk. "Not so fasht, buddy. Before I commence discushing nuclear physishks with you, my friend, I have three preliminary questions to asshk you."

"Okay, sir," says the bartender, "fire away."

"Okay, here's the firsht question. To the nearest quarter of an ounce, tell me the average statistical weight of a rooster turd."

"Well, let me see," the bartender ponders. "I'd say the average rooster turd weighs 1.5 ounces."

"Wrong!" says the drunk. "The correct answer is 2.3 ounces! Now, here's question number two. To the nearest half pound, tell me the average statistical weight of a gorilla turd."

"Okay," says the bartender, warming up to his assignment. "Let's see. I would say that the average gorilla turd weights 1.4 pounds."

"Wrong again, dummy," says the drunk. "The average gorilla turd weights less than half a pound. Now for the third and final question," says the drunk. "To the nearest full pound, what is the average statistical weight of a hippopotamus turd?"

"I would judge that the average hippopotamus turd weighs in at about 2.25 pounds," says the bartender, uneasily.

"Wrong again!" roars the drunk. "The average hippopotamus turd weighs 4.75 pounds!"

"Well, okay, so you stumped me," says the bartender. "Now can we proceed with our discussion of nuclear physics?"

"Are you kidding?" cries the drunk. "I'm supposed to engage in a discussion of nuclear physishks with you – when you don't know shit?"

67. STRANGER THAN FICTION.

A gentleman arrives at Fontainebleau Hotel in Miami Beach, checks in, and almost immediately dons a bathing suit, a robe, and saunters out to the pool deck.

He has barely plopped himself at poolside and immersed his alabaster white limbs into the sparkling waters when one of a bevy of aging divorcees spots him and makes a beeline for her latest prey.

With nerves all a-twitter, Mrs. Eisendrath quickly positions her ample posterior on the pool side immediately next to his and exclaims, "Velcome! Velcome, dahlink! You're new, aren't you? Just arrive today, right?"

"That's right, madam," replied the stranger.

"Mmmmmmm…I knew it!" exclaims Mrs. Eisendrath, "I can always tell. Look at you! Just look at you! Look how pale you are, dahlink. I mean, you are really, really pale! Where are you coming from?"

"I'm in from Ohio," says the taciturn stranger.

"Vell, you certainly couldn't have had much sun there, dahlink! I mean, you are really pale! How come? May I ask?"

"Well, you see, madam, if you must know…I've spent the last 17 years in the maximum security section of the Ohio State Penitentiary."

"Ooooooh!" squeals Mrs. Eisendrath. "That's exciting! May I ask what they sent you up for?"

"Well, if you must know, it was for the ax murder of my wife and five children."

Mrs. Eisendrath's face is bursting with delight. "That means you're single?"

68. CINDERELLA, HAVE A BALL.

Cinderella is sitting by her hearth in tatters, grimy, dejected. She is weeping uncontrollably. Suddenly her fairy godmother appears. "Cinderella, my child! Why are you crying?"

"I'm crying because my fucking wicked stepsisters went off to the ball and left me here to scrub floors!"

"Well, that's ridiculous. You, too, can go to the ball, my child! I'll see to that."

"That's fine for you to say, but I don't have a stitch to wear!" Cinderella bemoans as the tears continue to drip.

"Nonsense! We'll fix that!" And zap, the fairy godmother waves her wand and Cinderella is fully bedecked in a magnificent St. Laurent evening gown. Cinderella glances appreciatively at her new garb, but continues to cry.

"What's the matter now, my child?"

"I don't have any dancing shoes," the girl moans.

"Oh, that's easy. We can fix that pronto!" says the fairy godmother, who waves her wand again, producing two dainty Ferragamo glass slippers. But Cinderella continues to weep.

"What's the matter now, my child?"

"I have no way to get to the ball!" exclaims the young girl.

"No problem, sweetheart!" says the fairy godmother, whipping the wand again across the air and producing a magnificent coach, horses and attendants.

Still the young girl continues weeping.

"What the fuck is the matter with you, my child! You've got everything necessary to go to the ball. Now get the hell out of here!" says the fairy godmother. "Now why are you still crying?"

"Because there's still one more thing, Fairy Godmother. I'm having my period and those fucking wicked stepsisters of mine went off with all of my tampons."

"Oh, big deal! No problem whatsoever," exclaims the fairy godmother as she waves the wand in a graceful arc and produces a magnificent jeweled tampon. "Here. Insert this and be off with you and dry those tears."

Cinderella's face is radiant with joy as she inserts the tampon and heads for the coach. "Oh, thank you, Fairy Godmother. You're the greatest. You're just super. How can I ever thank you?"

"Don't thank me, my child — but there is one catch!"

"What's that, Fairy Godmother?" the girl asks.

"You have to be home by the stroke of midnight, or that tampon turns into a pumpkin," the fairy godmother admonishes.

"Oh, no problem, Fairy Godmother. No problem at all," says Cinderella as she trips off to the coach.

Several hours pass and Cinderella is now at the ball. Everyone is ga-ga over her beauty and she meets a handsome prince who has monopolized all of her dances. He waltzes her around the floor endlessly, gazing into her beautiful blue eyes. They are falling in love. She is enthralled. He is entranced.

Suddenly, she screeches to a halt on the dance floor and looks at her watch. It says ten minutes to twelve.

"Oh, my God! I must be going! I must leave right away!" exclaims Cinderella.

"Wait a minute! Wait a minute!" says the prince in total consternation. "You can't do this! Here we are, falling in love! You can't go now! I don't even know your name!"

"My name's Cinderella and I'm in the phone book," she says as she starts heading for the exit. "By the way, what's yours?" she calls over her shoulder as she races for the door.

"Peter Peter Pumpkineater!" yells the prince.

Suddenly Cinderella reels around on her glass slippers and exclaims, "Oh! In that case, I'll stay another hour!"

CHAPTER SIX

LIFE'S DEVASTATING MOMENTS

Personal Crisis Management Is An Art Form.

69. FRIGATEERING.

It's the 16th Century and a British naval frigate is patrolling Caribbean waters in search of pirates. The blue waters are serene, the breeze is stiff and the sun is sparkling. It's a perfect day to blast somebody out of the water.

Capt. Murgatroyd is standing erect on the bridge, itching for a fight. Suddenly, the seaman in the crow's nest bellows, "Pirate galleon at three miles, 20 degrees off the starboard bow!"

On the bridge, Murgatroyd claps his hands together, expands his chest and says to his first officer, "Ah-ha, at last we have a battle! Blimey! Quick, go down to my stateroom and bring me up my red jacket."

"Aye, sir," says the first officer and goes below. In a few moments, he returns with an elegant red jacket with embroidered collar and brass buttons. As he helps his captain don the garb, he asks, "If I might ask, sir, what is the purpose of the red jacket?"

"It's very simple, my son," says Murgatroyd. "In any sea battle, it is my custom to don a red jacket so that, in the event that I am injured and bleeding, my crew will never know."

"I see, sir," says the first officer. "I'm sorry to be so ignorant of your practices. This is my first cruise."

Standing there majestically with his telescope at the ready, the captain waits until the frigate closes upon the galleon from the rear, then he commands it to turn broadside and commands: "Fire all starboard guns." His crew emits a tremendous volley that cascades into the pirate galleon and blows it away. Murgatroyd glows with satisfaction. An hour later comes another call from the crow's nest: "Three pirate galleons, four miles, 30 degrees off the port bow." The captain swivels his telescope around. Two minutes later comes a call from the crow's nest: "Six pirate galleons at three miles, ten degrees off the starboard stern, approaching rapidly!" The captain swivels his telescope around to view the new threat.

A few moments later, a call comes from the crow's nest: "Seven more pirate galleons approaching quickly at 15 degrees off the port stern!" Murgatroyd swivels the telescope around again to view this new threat. After only a few moments more comes another call from the crow's nest: "Eight pirate galleons approaching rapidly, at two miles, ten degrees off the starboard bow!"

"First officer!"

"Yes, sir?"

"Bring me my brown pants."

70. LOVEMAKING MEETS INFLATION.

A drunk is sitting at the bar just off the main lounge of a house of prostitution in Las Vegas. He has been drunk all evening, and at the moment, he's blind drunk and deeply despondent.

The story behind his travail is simply that when he checked in with the house madam, already half-inebriated, he had spent most of his available funds on scotch, and had only a few dollars left for love. Taking pity on his penurious plight, the madam had an assistant produce a blow-up doll from a closet, inflate it, and sent it to him and assigned him a room upstairs with his new playmate.

Now he's in the depths of despair, sitting at the bar, crying into one last drink. A fellow patron notices him, comes up, puts a hand on his shoulder and says, "Why so sad, buddy?"

The drunk turns to him and says, "Oh, my God, I've been at the highesht and the lowesht this evening! I've been to heaven and to hell! They assigned me this fantastic girl who was the love of my life. We went up to the room and had a fantastic time. I had fallen deeply in love and she knew it. But then…when I tried to pin a corsage on her chesht …she suddenly farted and flew out the window."

71. LIFE'S NEXT CHAPTER.

Ginsburg is undergoing severe business reversals. He decides to take counsel with the Lord. Tonight, he makes contact.

"God, I really need some guidance. Two of my divisions are showing major sales declines. My West Coast warehouses are having shipping problems. Two of my best sales managers have fled to the competition. My idiots in quality control are going to cost me a major product recall. Those schleppers in R&D haven't come with a new product idea in a year. Cash flow is down to a trickle, and my creditors are beating down the gates. What do I do?"

A booming voice speaketh unto Ginsburg and says, "The answer, my son, can be found in the Talmud."

"The Talmud?"

"Yes, my son, the Talmud. Just place it on your windowsill tonight and tomorrow morning you will have the answer."

Baffled but compliant, Ginsburg retrieves the Talmud and carefully places it on the windowsill, so that its pages are gently flipping in the breeze.

The next morning, he rubs his eyes, leaps out of bed and dashes to the windowsill for the heavenly advice. He finds the Talmud open to Chapter XI.

72. TELLING IT LIKE IT IS.

Living in apartments on Bay Harbor Island in Biscayne Bay off of Miami Beach, four middle-aged ladies have been playing bridge together for 20 years.

On this particular afternoon, after the final card is played and tea is served, Blanche suddenly arises and says, "Girls…girls! I can't stand it any longer. I just can't stand it. We've been playing bridge together for 20 years, have been friends for 20 years, and all that time I have fought off the urge to confess. But I have a confession and I have to give it to you today. I can't wait a moment longer!"

A hush fell over the group and her friends gather close, with quizzical expressions. Blanche continues, "All this time you thought that I was a normal friend, but I'm not. Guess what? I'm a kleptomaniac! Yes, I'm a kleptomaniac. Of course, I've never ever stolen one thing from any of you, but I want you to know that I have always been a compulsive kleptomaniac, and I simply must confess it to you." An awkward silence falls over the group, but then each of the others extends her hands compassionately to Blanche and nods in affection. Then within less than a minute, Florence suddenly jumps out of her chair, raises her hands and says, "Girls…girls! Just a minute! If this is confession time, I too have a confession to make, and I want all of you to hear it. After all these years that I've kept it bottled inside me, I have to let you know. Guess what? Guess what? All these years that you known me, you never knew that I, Florence, am a nymphomaniac. Yes, a nymphomaniac. Of course, obviously, I've never gone after any of your husbands, but I just can't help myself, and I've been a nymphomaniac all of my adult life."

The other three are getting into the spirit of the thing now and once again nod understandingly at this new revelation.

In less than another minute, Sadie leaps out of her chair and says, "Ladies, ladies, ladies! Hold everything! I'm getting into the same spirit, and I want you to hear my confession, too. For 20 years we've been close friends, and in all that time, none of you ever had the slightest inkling that I am a lesbian. Yes, a lesbian. But it's true. Of course, I've never gone after any of your daughters, but I have lived this incredible double life and kept if all from you."

Once again, there is an outpouring of affection and consolation.

Finally, Sophie leaps to her feet, throws her arms in the air and screams, "Okay, okay, okay! As long as everyone's confessing, I'm confessing, too. I am a yenta! And I can't wait to get home to start telling everybody!"

73.   COMFORT OF CONVICTION.

A world-famed stock market manipulator is finally brought to justice, convicted and sentenced to a minimum security prison in Southern California.

Because of his pre-eminence in the world of white collar crime, he is given a regal welcome by the warden, who escorts him on a personally conducted tour of the facilities.

As the two walk the lushly planted grounds, the warden asks, "Tell me, Mr. Jones, do you play tennis?"

"Yes, I do."

"Then you're going to love Mondays, because every Monday we have a marvelous round robin tournament on these superb Har-tru all-weather courts. And lunch is served right here at courtside during the midday break."

"Gee, how wonderful!"

"And Mr. Jones, how about golf? Do you play golf?" asks the warden.

"Yes, I love golf."

"Good, then you're going to love Tuesdays and Thursdays, because on Tuesdays and Thursdays we have a wonderful golf tournament and matched foursomes, complete with caddies and golf carts provided, and you can see how well-maintained our fairways are."

"Wow, beautiful!" exclaims Jones.

"And how about bridge? Are you a bridge player?"

"Oh, yes! I've been a lifelong bridge addict."

"Wonderful! Then you're going to love Fridays, because every Friday here on the terrace we have a duplicate bridge tournament that is conducted on these umbrella tables, and with a buffet lunch served."

"Gee, that's terrific! I never thought prison would be like this. But wait a minute…what happens on Wednesdays?"

"Well, Mr. Jones, that's a special day. Are you gay?"

"No."

"That's a shame. You're going to hate Wednesdays!"

74. JUMPING FOR JOY.

Isaac and Benny are history's first two Jewish paratroopers. They are sent to the Army's training school at Ft. Bragg, North Carolina, where they have now spent a month in basic preflight indoctrination. Now it's time for their first jump.

As the two roommates leave their quarters this morning to report to two separate jump platoons, their faces are ashen white and they are visibly shaking. They embrace, give each other a dose of courage, and agree to meet at the mess hall at noon to relate their first war story.

Benny is already slurping some soup at the mess hall when Isaac appears, looking more like a ghost than ever. He hobbles over to the table and takes a seat.

"Boy, Isaac! I thought I had a scary, terrible morning until I took one look at you. What happened? You look like you've been through an entire campaign!"

Isaac, his limbs still shaking, pulls his chair closer to his friend, bends his head lower, and in a weak whimper begins whispering: "Oy, Benny, it was awful! It was the most devastating experience of my life! There we were, all lined up, and they start pushing these guys out the door one by one! Well, Benny, I just lost my nerve. I couldn't do it, so I quietly slipped back to the tail section of the plane and hid, all rolled up in a ball. After a few minutes, I felt a huge hand on my shoulder, and I heard the words of the big master sergeant saying, 'Hey, you little Jewish shit! What do you think you's doing? If y'all don't get yo' ass out that door in ten seconds, I'm going to yank down those pants and take my humongous organ and ram it right up yo' cowardly Jewish rectum!"

"Oh, my God," whispered Benny to his sobbing friend. "So, did you jump?"

"Yes, a little."

75. BIG MOTHER.

In a fit of sheer panic, Karen Rabinowitz dials her bedroom telephone.

"Hello?"

Bursting into tears, Karen exclaims in an escalating tone, "Mother, it's me. You won't believe it. You just won't believe it. I have one kid down with bronchitis and another one with the 'flu. That bastard husband of mine is on another business trip this week. Dr. Silverman's phone doesn't answer. The drug store is closed. I have nothing in the icebox because the Bermans ate us out of house and home last night. I haven't been able to get out of here because these two brats are driving me crazy. My back is killing me. I have a migraine headache, and what do you think? Lena didn't show up today, so the entire place is a mess. Mother, I'm about to kill myself."

"Oh, my God, darling. My poor sweetheart. My poor baby. That's terrible. What a mess. What a mess. Well, don't worry. I'm canceling my bridge game immediately. I'm marching into the kitchen and making a huge pot of chicken matzo ball soup, which is the best possible cure for the kids. Then I'm stopping at Bloomberg's pharmacy and buying out the place. Don't worry. I'll pick up every remedy I can for each kid, plus some liniment for your back, plus some nice Tylenol for your headache. Then I'm stopping at the A&P and picking up everything you could possibly need for dinner tonight, breakfast and lunch tomorrow for you and the kids, plus dinner tomorrow night. And don't worry, it will be the finest of everything. I know what each of you likes and I'm especially hunting for those little raspberries that I know you love, and while I'm at it, I'll find the latest book for you to read to take your mind off all this and a toy for each of the kids. What's more, I'm going to do all of this in the coming hour and be there in time to fix dinner for all of you, put the kids to bed, and then give your back a nice rubdown with the liniment. After that, I'm cleaning up the house spic and span so everything's in shape and who needs Lena? So don't worry your pretty head, my darling. Help is on the way!"

"Oh, Mother! Do you really mean it?"

"Of course, my kinder. What else are mothers for?"

"Oh, you are a Godsend! That would be such an incredible mitzvah, Mother," Karen sobs. "It's almost like as long as I have you, who needs Morris?"

"Morris? Who's this Morris?"

"My husband, Mother. My husband Morris."

"What are you talking Morris, darling? You know your husband is David!"

"Wait a minute – is this 734-2817?"

"No, this is 734-2816!"

"Oh, my God! Oh, my God," Karen screams. "Does that mean you're not coming?"

76. MAKING THE GRADE.

While Hortense is at the wheel, driving downtown from the suburbs, her ten-year-old daughter is in the back seat playing with her mother's purse.
"Hey, Mom!"
"What is it, Lillith?"
"Mom…now I know why you got a divorce!"
"What are you talking about, Lillith? And stay out of my purse!"
"Mom…I discovered why you got a divorce! I'm looking at your driver's license. You got an "F" in sex!"

77. IMMOBILIZATION.

It is the celebrated evening of the North American debut of the great Pavlova. There is standing room only at the Lincoln Center. The packed house tingles with excitement. The audience is enthralled as the celebrated ballerina stages an unforgettable performance.

It is now the climax of the final scene, and as the audience audibly gasps with increasing fervor, the great Pavlova dazzles her fans with ever more stupendous feats of grace and agility.

Finally, as the music reaches its ultimate crescendo, her brawny partner, Igor, hurls the great Pavlova an incredible ten feet into the air and, like some miraculous bird-creature, with beautiful legs pointed fore and aft, she plummets back to the stage, executing an absolutely perfect split. Her hands are raised gaily above her head in a final salute while her face beams at her audience, eyes a-flutter.

The impact of the scene is titanic. As the curtain descends and Pavlova remains in her split position with her partner gazing upon her, the audience is totally awe-struck. After a moment of stunned silence, it erupts in unison into a frantic burst of screaming applause. No one has ever witnessed a ballet finale like this. The thundering applause gathers momentum. The curtain rises. Igor turns and bows, then graciously gestures to Pavlova, who remains on the stage, motionless, in her split position, beaming at her admiring fans. A torrent of roses descends upon the stage in tribute to her greatness.

The curtain descends again. The applause grows to an even greater intensity. The curtain rises. Igor bows again. Pavlova remains on the stage, motionless in her split position. The curtain descends.

The curtain rises, more roses cascade upon the stage. Igor bows again. His partner remains motionless in her split position. In ten more curtain calls, the audience witnesses the identical scene. Finally, as the applause subsides, the curtain remains down and Igor calls to his partner, still motionless in her split position. "Pavlova? Pavlova? My darling! Are you all right? Pavlova! What's the matter? Are you paralyzed? Are you hurt? Why can't you move? Pavlova!"

With a graceful gesture of her hand, the prima ballerina beckons her partner close. Igor immediately runs to her side, stoops down and exclaims, "Pavlova! What happened?"

"Come closer, Igor. Closer," Pavlova whispers.

"What is it, my darling?" Igor says in horrified apprehension.

"Rock me, rock me, Igor," she whispers, "and break the suction!"

78. SPECIAL DELIVERY.

Don Giovanni is one of the great capo di capo of the Brooklyn Mafioso.

He is sitting at his desk in his study within his palatial and well-fortified home. This morning he calls into the study his faithful henchman, Georgio, and his faithful bagman, Luigi.

"Georgio," says Don Giovanni, "I have a special assignment for you. My friend Don Bernardo in Milano has justa paid off his debt to me of $5 million in cash, and dis sum is contained in the a black briefcase dat will be arriving at Pier 47 on the Hudson River at exactly 11 a.m. dis morning. I want you to hava Luigi run down to da pier and pick up dat briefcase and bring it back to me. Capiche?"

Luigi is sitting there in the room, but understands nothing because he is a deaf-mute. It was for that very reason that Don Giovanni selected him as his personal bagman, so that if he were ever apprehended, he could never sing.

However, Georgio is skilled and fluent in sign language and is the personal translator, mentor and custodian of Luigi. Georgio turns to him and, with deft finger and hand motions, says, "Luigi, the boss wantsa you go down to Pier 47 on the Hudson River where the black briefcase is arriving from Milano. You are to bring dat briefcase back to da boss. Datsa da assignment. Capiche?"

Luigi nods obediently. Then the little messenger walks briskly out of the house, hops on his black Harley-Davidson parked in the driveway and roars off for Manhattan. Several hours later, Luigi still hasn't returned and Don Giovanni is pacing his study. Georgio is pacing the hall outside. The clock keeps ticking away. Still nothing. Finally, a little after 4 p.m., Luigi pulls into the driveway and runs into the house, bearing the long-awaited black briefcase. Georgio escorts him into the boss's study, and he ceremoniously places the black briefcase on the desk. In a vile mood, Don Giovanni impatiently opens the black briefcase, looks inside, turns it upside down, shakes it, and slams it down on the desk.

"Empty! Nothing!" the boss thunders. "Whatsa da big deal! Is disa some kind of a joke!" His face is turning purple.

Georgio begins to perspire and turns to Luigi, with fingers beginning to fly in every direction, saying, "Luigi, da boss is not amused. Is disa some kind of a gag? What happened to da money?"

Luigi just sits there with a blank, helpless look on his face. Then with his brow furrowed into an expression of agonized innocence, Luigi responds with his own sign language: "Georgio…I'ma don't know nothing! I'ma just did like you tell me to do. I wenta to da Pier 47 and I pick up da briefcase and bring it right back to da boss here."

Trembling, Georgio turns to his superior and says, "Boss, Luigi says he does just like we tell him to. He goesa to da pier, picks up the briefcase and brings it back here."

The veins in Don Giovanni's forehead are now bulging and his eyes are mere slits. He opens his desk drawer, removes a .357 Magnum pistol and slowly walks over to where Luigi is sitting. He places the muzzle directly against Luigi's temple and cocks the gun. Then he speaks, "Georgio, tell your friend that he has 60 seconds to tell us exactly what happened to da money or I blow his fucking brains out!"

Georgio turns to Luigi and pleads, "Luigi…Luigi…da boss is now very agitated. As you can see, he really wantsa da information! Da boss say dat you got 60 seconds to tell us what happened to da money or else da boss blows your fucking brains out!"

Luigi sits there stiffly for a few moments, but then rivulets of perspiration begin streaming down his face. His cheeks twitch a few times, he glances at Georgio, then a sideways glance at the pistol, then staring back at Georgio. Finally, he raises his fingers to speak: "Okay, okay, Georgio, okay. I'll tell you…okay, I took the money and hid it in Lock Box Number 3789 at LaGuardia and I hid the key on the upper shelf of my closet at my apartment. I'ma sorry! I'ma sorry!"

"Well, Georgio?" says Don Giovanni with a grimace. "What did Luigi tell us?"

"Boss," Georgio quietly reports, "Luigi say…you don't hava da balls to pull da fucking trigger!"

CHAPTER SEVEN

SPORTS

The Enthusiastic Athletics Supporter.

79. THE FUN CLUB.

A police detective and two police sergeants break into an apartment. There, they find a well-known lady golf pro standing over the dead body of her husband, prostrate on the floor. His head is bashed in and she is standing over him, holding a bloody eight-iron.

The lawmen are stunned. Finally, the detective says, "Madam, did you do this deed?"

"Yes, I did. The bastard deserved it."

"And did you use that eight-iron?" says the detective.

"Yes, I did."

"How many times did you hit him?"

"I don't know…five…six…maybe seven…put me down for a five."

80. SALE OF THE SEASON.

Himmelman is in his first day as a retail salesman at Wal-Mart.

Late in the morning, the floor manager is somewhat irritated to find that his newest employee has been tied up for two hours with one customer, a balding middle-aged gentleman. He calls Himmelman over for a private conversation.

"Himmelman, what do you think you're doing? You've wasted almost two hours with this one customer. That isn't the way we do things here. This is a high-volume business. Understand? We hafta bring 'em in, sell 'em something and then get 'em out. Now tell me, has he bought anything yet?"

"Yes, sir."

"Well, that's good. What's the merchandise total so far?"

"Thus far, sir, it's a little over $112,000."

"What?? How is that possible?"

"I started out, sir, by showing him a fishing rod, and then I explained that he could be even better if he upgraded to one of our deluxe rods and special tackle. Then I told him that he'd need a least a dozen different types of lure. Then I suggested that rather than stand at the end of the pier and cast, he could catch much more if he was out on the lake in a rowboat, and I then showed him our deluxe aluminum skiff, which he further agreed to buy. Then we added to the list an elegant set of rain gear, a high-quality tackle box and one of our very chic picnic baskets."

"I see."

"Then I suggested that he not spend the time and energy to row his boat around the lake, but instead invest in one of our beautiful new 200 horsepower Johnson outboard motors, complete with fuel tank and accessories. Lastly, I suggested he buy our three-year warranty policy covering all equipment."

"Wow," says the floor manager. "That's incredible! This guy must be quite the sports fanatic!"

"Not really, sir. In fact, he's never been fishing before."

"Never fished?"

"No, sir. In fact, he only came in to buy a box of Tampax. I told him, 'Well, since you're not going to be doing anything for the coming week, why not go fishing?'"

81. THE REMEDY.

A lady golfer storms into the pro shop and demands to see the golf pro. In a short while, he emerges and says, "Yes, madam?"
"You have a very dangerous golf course here! I just got a bee sting!"
"Where, madam?"
"Between the first and second holes."
"Madam, your stance is too wide."

82. MENTAL SYMBIOSIS.

A daredevil tightrope walker is performing an amazing stunt. He is traversing a thin wire stretched between the top of New York's Chrysler Building on 42nd Street and the MetLife Building two blocks away.

Holding his balance pole and carefully navigating the wire as he edges forward, he is the portrait of equanimity.

Meanwhile, down below, in a lonely alley off of 44th Street, another young man is standing with his back against a brick wall, receiving oral sex from a 92-year-old woman.

In an incredibly telepathic communion, at that single moment, one thought flashed through the mind of both men simultaneously: "Don't look down."

83. BULLSEYE.

A woman is golfing on the fairway and hits a ball with a tremendous slice. The ball zooms right into a man's groin, he grasps his hands together in agony, doubles over and collapses on the adjacent fairway.

The woman is mortified and immediately sprints over to the next fairway to apologize and comfort the man. "I'm so terribly sorry about this. I have a hard time correcting my slice. I apologize profusely. By the way, I'm a physical therapist and perhaps I might be able to make it feel better."

He rolls over and consents to her offer of humanitarian first aid. He lays there for ten minutes while she works on his testicles, supplying every bit of therapeutic expertise at her command.

Finally, after ten minutes, she asks, "Well, now, does that feel better?"

"Yes, that feels great…but my thumb still hurts like hell."

84. FAIRWAY CHATTER.

A highly diversified foursome was walking down the fairway. There was a man in his fifties, another in his sixties, another in his seventies and another in his eighties.

As they strolled through the grass, the 50-year-old said to the others, "Fellas, I'm really feeling my age. I can hardly swing this club anymore. What's it like to grow older?"

"Well, my young friend, I have to tell you that the sixties are the worst age to experience," says the golfer in his sixties. "You always feel like you hafta pee and most of the time you stand there and nothing comes out."

"I agree that that becomes a problem," says the man in his seventies. "But when you're my age, you have a hard time with bowel movements as well. You take laxatives, you eat bran, you sit on the toilet all day, and you wait and wait."

"You guys have it easy," says the 85-year-old. "Wait 'til you get up into the eighties like me."

"Even more trouble peeing?" asks the man in his fifties.

"No. Matter of fact, I pee every morning at 6 a.m. I pee like a racehorse. No problem whatsoever."

"Well, then, you must have great problems with bowel movements," says the man in his fifties.

"No. In fact, I have one every morning at 6:30 a.m." says the 85-year-old.

With exasperation, the man in his fifties says, "If you pee every morning at 6 a.m. and crap every morning at 6:30, it sounds like things get a lot easier in the eighties. What's so bad about that routine?"

His elderly friend replies, "I don't get out of bed until 7."

85. THE NEW DISCIPLINE.

Bill Clinton is on the golf course, playing a round with three of his favorite cronies. He is wearing one of his customary short sleeve Lacoste t-shirts.

As they walk down the first fairway, his buddy Horace notices something strange. While attired in perfectly standard golfing dress, the former president has a pair of female panties wrapped around his left bicep.

None of the foursome has the temerity to question this bizarre accessory, and several holes are played. Finally, on the eighth hole, Horace works up the courage and says, "My curiosity has become overpowering, Bill. What on Earth is that wrapped around your bicep?"

Clinton smiles and says, "It's a patch. I'm trying to quit."

86. ARCHEOLOGICAL TREASURE.

Near downtown Warsaw, a Victorian-era apartment building is under demolition.

In the process, the construction crew is stunned to find a human skeleton wedged between the drywall of the former living room and the brick structure of the building.

By checking dental records and DNA samples, the authorities are able to ascertain with positive confirmation that this skeleton belonged to none other than Lech Polansky, the 1932 Polish National Hide-and-Seek Champion.

87. ONE UP.

It's a slow day at the golf club, and this morning at the first tee show up only a young man and a beautiful lady. There is no foursome available, so the golf pro pairs up the two strangers. They both agree to play 18 holes together. They both execute nice drives, and they are now walking down the first fairway together. The woman asks the gentleman if he would like to play for stakes equaling $100 per hole. He readily agrees to the wager.

However, his enthusiasm soon wanes. At the end of three holes, he is down $300. At the end of seven holes, he is down $700. And after putting in on the ninth green, he is down $900. The woman is a whiz, and he realizes that he is being taken to the cleaner's. It is a major hustle.

As the pair walks off the ninth green, the woman turns to him and says, "Look, I'm terribly embarrassed. I feel very badly about taking all this money from you. Let me at least compensate by offering to go behind those bushes over there and give you five minutes of oral sex."

The young man is stunned at first, then warms to the idea and shrugs his shoulders, nods and readily accepts the consolation prize.

Later, the pair then tees off on the 10th hole and continues to play the back nine. The woman's prowess is awesome. By the 18th green, she is $1,800 ahead. Her opponent is entirely decimated. As they putt in on the 18th hole, she once again puts a hand on his shoulder and says, "Oh, I'm so sorry. I feel so badly. This is just terrible. Please let me make it up to you. The least I can do is offer to go over there behind those bushes and give you a bit more oral sex." Again, he readily agrees to this second consolation prize, and they stroll behind the bushes. In the process of that encounter, and in the throes of his passion, he rips off her dress and, to his overwhelming shock, he discovers that she is the owner of male genitals.

"Why, you bastard!" he screams.

"What's the matter?" his companion asks.

"What's the matter? For 18 holes you've been teeing off from the ladies' tees!"

88.   DON'T BE CREWED.

One day, the provost of the Yeshiva University, a highly autocratic rabbi, decides that after all these years, Yeshiva should finally get into intercollegiate athletics.

He summons into his study his faithful assistant Mendelssohn, and exclaims," Mendelssohn! I've decided it's about time we get this university into the real world and start competing in intercollegiate athletics. However, I have a problem. Those tight bastards on our administrative committee have given me almost no budget for this sort of thing. Therefore, here is your mission."

"Yes, Rabbi?"

"Fine me the one sport that we can get into for just a few dollahs. I vant a sport that is respectable and I vant a sport that can blend us into the Eastern Ivy League atmosphere. In other words, it has to be chic but cheap!"

A day later, Mendelssohn returns to the rabbi's study with a cunning smirk. "Rabbi, I think I have your answer. I think I have our sport."

"So?"

"Crew."

"Chruuuu? Vat's chruuuu?"

"Crew. You know, Rabbi, crew racing. A bunch of boys rowing a boat down the river against a competing team."

"So? Vat does it take?"

"Very economical, Rabbi. Lowest budget possible. All we need to invest is a few dollars to buy a used boat, eight sets of oars and a few skimpy uniforms – and we're in business! And it's very, very respectable!"

"No kidding? Okay, let's do it. Make the investment and assemble the team! Yeshiva is competing!"

The Yeshiva nine are assembled and they practice on the East River for three months. At last, they are ready for competition, and as luck would have it, they draw as their first match Harvard University on the Charles. The race takes place as scheduled and the next morning, Benny Birnbaum, captain of the Yeshiva team, enters the Rabbi's study.

"Vell, Benny," the rabbi beams, "how did we do yesterday?"

"Rabbi, I'm sorry to report that we lost. In fact, we were totally trounced – by 13 boat-lengths! But confidentially, Rabbi, Harvard cheated!"

"Vat? You say Harvard cheated?"

"Yes, Rabbi. They had eight guys rowing and only one guy yelling!"

89. SORELY MISSED.

A Texan and his wife pay $5,000 for two seats on the 50-yard line to watch the Dallas Cowboys compete in the Super Bowl.

As the couple takes their seats, they notice an empty seat to their right and adjacent to that seat is a diminutive Mr. Schmendrik. The game commences and the Texas couple becomes increasingly disconcerted by the empty seat. Finally, in the second quarter, the husband leans over and says to Mr. Schmendrik, "Excuse me, mah friend, but we couldn't help but notice this empty seat. You must have paid the same $5,000 we did for those two seats and we're amazed that you allowed one to go empty."

"Vell, you're right. I did pay the same $5,000 because my wife and I had been planning for months to see the Super Bowl. But unfortunately, she passed away."

"Well, pardner, we're awful sorry to hear that. But it's hard for us to believe that you didn't have one friend who would love to join you for the Super Bowl and have that seat."

"Vell, I really don't. Unfortunately, they're all at the funeral."

CHAPTER EIGHT

MEDICINE

Here's To The Hype And Critical Oath.

90. SUBLIMATION.

A young doctor is laying on the couch, attended by a prominent psychiatrist. It is his first visit.

The psychiatrist decides to go right to the heart of the matter. What's the underlying psychotic problem?

The patient spills it out. "Doctor, I'm just tremendously bothered, embarrassed and emotionally distraught because I keep sleeping with my patients."

The psychiatrist says, "My advice, Doctor, is to simply try to let it go."

"I try. I really try. But please remember, I'm a veterinarian."

91. HEART OF THE MATTER.

A prominent cardiac surgeon visits the garage where a mechanic is in the process of overhauling the doctor's Harley-Davidson.

Sitting there on the floor of the garage with the motorcycle engine disassembled and parts scattered around him, the mechanic peers up at his customer, grimaces and views the challenging task before him. He sighs and mutters, "You know, Doctor, in all honesty, let me tell you that I find this situation depressing. There's just no equality in this world. Consider that you're a heart surgeon, earning hundreds of thousands of dollars a year for what you do. Now, consider also that here I am, operating delicately and skillfully on the precious pistons, valves and tappets in the very heart of your motorcycle. And yet, I make a lousy $27,000 a year. Is there something wrong with this picture?"

The doctor smiles, shrugs his shoulders and says, "Well, consider this. Have you ever tried to do an overhaul with the engine running?"

READ AT YOUR OWN RISQUE!

92. CLEAR VISION.

Mr. Linowicz was in the doctor's office having an eye exam.

"Can you read this, sir?" He flashes letters across the screen. They are: C Z W I X N O S T.

"Can I read it?" says Linowicz. "I KNOW the guy!"

93. PREMATURE EXPIRATION.

Irving is in a private room in the hospital. He isn't doing well. He is sinking rapidly.

His family is gathered around him in a desperate effort to comfort him. His rabbi is also there.

Suddenly, Irving raises his hand. He's unable to speak, but through sign language, he communicates urgently that he needs a piece of paper and a pen. Standing next to him at beside, the rabbi immediately produces a piece of note paper and writing implement. Laying there in great pain and turmoil, Irving scribbles a note furiously, then hands it quickly to the rabbi. Just as he hands the note over, Irving turns blue and quietly expires.

Thinking that the note is some type of last wish or expression that perhaps should be read at the funeral service, the rabbi holds the note and deposits it in his pocket.

Three days later, as he is preparing to conduct the funeral service and delivery of a eulogy, the rabbi remembers the note, digs in his pocket, pulls out the note and reads it:

"SCHMUCK! MOVE! YOU'RE STANDING ON MY AIRHOSE!"

94. THE NEWEST CPR.

Mr. Wicnzewski's wife has been in a coma for months. She remains in an ICU under close observation.

One day a nurse is bathing Mrs. Wicnzewski and happens to be washing the vaginal area when she notices a sudden reaction on the heart monitor. It is going beep...beep...beep...beep, beep, beep, beep, beep, beep.

She immediately summons the doctor and relates the incident. The doctor says, "Hmmmmmmn. A very interesting development, nurse. This gives me an idea! I think we shall try a little experiment. Get Mr. Wicnzewski over here right away!"

Mr. Wicnzewski arrives from the office and the doctor says, "Mr. Wicnzewski, when our nurse was bathing your wife today and washed her vaginal area, we noted a very positive response on the heart monitor. I'd like your cooperation in helping us with a little experiment. I'd like you to go in there and give your wife ten minutes of oral sex. It's just possible that we can pull her out of this coma."

Mr. Wicnzewski nods, shrugs his shoulders and obediently enters the ICU while the nurse and doctor remain on the outside, observing the heart monitor with bated breath. After a few minutes, they see the monitor going beep...beep...beep...beep...beep, beep, beep, beep, beep, beep, beeeeeeeeeeeeeep!

"Oh, my Lord!" cries the doctor. "That's a flatline! She's dead!"

The doctor rushes into the ICU and confronts the stupefied husband. "Mr. Wicnzewski!. What on Earth happened?"

"I dunno," replied the husband. "I think she choked to death."

95. DON'T ASK, DON'T TELL.

The young man is ushered into the doctor's office, sits down and when the doctor says, "What can I do for you, young man," the patient replies, "Doctor, I want you to test me and see if I'm gay."

"Okay," says the doctor, "drop your pants." The patient complies.

"The doctor proceeds to don a rubber glove and insert an index finger up the patient's rectum. "Now, count to ten"

"One…one and a half…two…two and a half…"

96. HMO IS WHERE THE HEART IS.

In 1993, as part of her firsthand research to develop her national health care legislation, First Lady Hillary Clinton is touring a major hospital complex. Accompanied by the administrator of the facility, Mrs. Clinton is enjoying her tour and taking copious notes. All of a sudden, as she walks with him down the next corridor, she is startled to see a male patient in a private room being given oral sex by a female nurse, on her knees.

"My God!" cries out the First Lady. "What's going on there?"

"Well, Mrs. Clinton," the administrator confides in a low tone, "that's the special therapy that we must administer to certain patients in this section. That man is afflicted with a malady that is ESS – Excessive Semen Syndrome. It's a disease in which the patient suffers a rapid and immense buildup of surplus semen in his body, and if he is not properly drained twice a day, he will die."

The First Lady stares back in utter amazement and tries to maintain her composure. She can barely do more than nod her head weakly. She and the administrator continue walking a few paces further and then turn a corner of the corridor. Suddenly, she sees in front of her another male patient in a wheelchair sitting alone in the hallway, systematically masturbating and ejaculating all over the wall.

"What in the world!" Mrs. Clinton exclaims. "Now I've seen everything! This is incredible! Is this whole place crazy?"

"Now, Mrs. Clinton, please stay calm. You must understand that most of the patients in this ward are afflicted by that same disease, Excess Semen Syndrome. Each of them must have relief twice a day."

"I understand," says Mrs. Clinton, "but why is that first patient in a private room receiving oral sex from a nurse, while this poor man out here is masturbating in the hallway?"

"Well, you see, Mrs. Clinton, the man in the private room has private insurance, while the man out here is in the HMO."

97. DIABOLICAL DIAGNOSIS.

The good-looking young physician sits down with his patient and reports, "Well, Mr. Brown, we've completed all the lab tests and I now have a conclusive reading for you. Basically, I have good news and bad news."

"Okay, Doc, give me the bad news."

"Well, Mr. Brown, your condition is definitely terminal and you have about six months to live."

The patient takes the news very hard, breaks into uncontrollable sobs and is comforted by the doctor for several minutes. Finally, the patient pulls himself together enough to say, "Okay, Doc, now give me the good news."

"Mr. Brown, take a look out into our office bay. So you see that row of desks? Now, do you see that third nurse on the left? I mean the one with the huge breasts and small waist, the one with the raven hair cascading down her back...you see what one I mean? The truly gorgeous one?"

The patient wipes his eyes and says incredulously, "Yes, Doc, I think I see the one."

"Well, I'm fucking her."

98. THE DISCRIMINATING PATIENT.

Schwartz has had a triple bypass and is now convalescing nicely at Mass General Hospital. But one day, without warning, he demands that he be transferred to Beth Israel Hospital down the road. The doctors comply with his wishes.

Now he is convalescing nicely at Beth Israel and the hospital's chief cardiologist pays a visit to Schwartz's private room.

"Good morning, Mr. Schwartz," says the doctor. "Do you mind if I ask you a frank, personal question?"

"No, Doctor, go right ahead."

"Well, Mr. Schwartz, help us to understand something. There you were, after a successful bypass surgery, recuperating in good style at Mass General – the premier hospital in all of New England – and yet you interrupt everybody and demand that you be transferred to our little hospital. Of course, we're flattered, but...Mr. Schwartz, why are you here?"

"Vell, Doctor, I'll tell you. Yes, there I was at Mass General, with the finest facilities. My room has space age technology, the state-of-the-art in everything...I couldn't complain about the amenities...pushbutton TV ...a VCR...a stereo system...everything at my fingertips. And then there was the gorgeous view. I certainly couldn't complain about that. And then there were those marvelous nurses. Nothing to complain about them. They were gorgeous. They were attentive. They were shapely. They were fabulous. And then there was the cuisine. I certainly couldn't complain about that. Green turtle soup with sherry...pasta with white truffles...Tournedos Perigourdine! And it was served fast and hot and superbly."

"But then, Mr. Schwartz, why are you here?"

"Why am I here? Because here I can complain!"

99. CORPUS DELECTABLE.

Gus and Cornelius are two attendants at the city morgue. Gus is age 65 and Cornelius is age 25. Together, they work as a team.

This morning, a new corpse has just arrived. As they prepare him to go into his assigned drawer, they remove the sheet to reveal an extremely well-endowed young man.

"Wow!" says Cornelius. "Will you look at that thing?"

"I don't know," mutters Gus, "that's not so impressive. In fact, I have one just like it."

"What?" exclaims Cornelius. "You've got to be kidding. You have one that big?"

"You're talking big," Gus replies. "I'm talking dead."

100. HOME REMEDY.

A middle-aged woman is walking up and down the aisles of a drugstore. Every couple of moments, she is going, "Ah-choooo!" in a loud sneeze, followed immediately by, "Ohhhhhhhh…ahhhhhhhhhh!"

For several minutes this series continues, with "ah-choooo!" followed immediately by "Ohhhhhhhh…ahhhhhhhhhh!"

Finally the druggist comes up to the woman and says, "Madam, what's the matter with you?"

"Well, you see, I have this strange allergy. And every time I sneeze, I have an orgasm."

"Hmmmn. I see," says the druggist. "What are you taking for it?"

"Pollen."

101. THE PRESCRIPTION.

Abe Glickstein is taking his wife, Blanche, to the doctor.

Abe sits in the waiting room and reads a magazine. Blanche is summoned into the examination room by a nurse.

"And what seems to be the problem, Mrs. Glickstein?" asks the doctor after she has disrobed.

"I don't know, Doctor. I just seem to be feeling not mineself lately. Kind of out of sorts. Kind of schvach."

"Well, let me give you a complete physical and we'll find the problem," says the doctor.

He then proceeds to administer a complete physical and at the end, states, "Mrs. Glickstein, this is a real mystery. You are in excellent physical condition. I can find absolutely nothing wrong with you. Let's talk further and see if we can identify the source of the problem. Tell me about your sex life."

"Sex life? Vat sex life?"

"You know, I mean, please describe to me the kind of sex life you have with Mr. Glickstein. What goes on?"

"Vell, not much."

"Well, Mrs. Glickstein, tell me how often you have it."

"Vell, maybe every six months," says Mrs. Glickstein.

"Well, that ridiculous for a woman of your middle age," explains the doctor. "Let's see if you have some problem with the sex act itself. Hop up here on the examination table and I'll just try you out and see if you have any inhibitions, phobias or physical incompatibilities with the male of the species."

Obediently, Mrs. Glickstein complies with the experiment, climbs up on the examination table and is immediately mounted by the doctor, without bothering to remove his medical garb. After the act is completed, the doctor puts himself back together and asks Mrs. Glickstein to get dressed. After she does, the physician asks her to be seated once again in his office.

Mrs. Glickstein, based on my examination, I must conclude that you are a first-rate specimen of American womanhood, totally devoid of any sexual dysfunction. Now let's call your husband in here."

Mr. Glickstein is summoned by the nurse and led into the physician's office. He is asked to have a seat next to Mrs. Glickstein.

"Now, Mr. Glickstein, I have given your wife a thorough physical examination. I have concluded that she is in perfect physical condition and suffers only from a lack of frequency in sexual activity. In fact, I even tried her out myself right here on the examination table to be sure of my conclusion. She has no sexual dysfunction, performs perfectly, and needs only a greater frequency of sex."

"Greater frequency? How often?" murmurs Glickstein, peering at the doctor over his glasses, then looking nervously sideways at his wife.

"Oh, I'd say twice a week, at least," says the doctor.

"Twice a week? What days?" asks Glickstein.

"What days? I don't know – let's say Tuesdays and Thursdays," states the doctor.

Glickstein thinks for a moment and then finally announces, "Well… Tuesdays, I can bring her in, but Thursdays she'll have to take the bus."

102. THE DOCTOR IS OUT.

Dr. Lionel Cohen was a compulsive philanderer.

The first time that his wife discovered his dalliances and nailed him on the incident, he paced up and down the bedroom, throwing up his hands in great shame and chagrin.

"Yes, honey! Yes, honey! You've got me. I'm guilty as sin. You are dead right. I'm dead wrong. I yielded to temptation and I'm sorry. All I can tell you is that she wasn't half as good as you are in bed. In fact, speaking not only as your husband and lover but as a medical doctor, I would have to state emphatically that you are the most alluring, most erotic, most satisfying specimen of American womanhood that exists today!"

The second time that the good doctor is caught red-handed in yet another such dalliance, he has the same response when he is called upon the carpet by his wife in the bedroom that evening.

"Once again, my love, I hang my head in shame, utter shame. I am thoroughly guilty and have no excuse. For the record is what I have stated before. As a husband, lover and medical doctor, these experiences only convince me, beyond a shadow of a doubt, that your expertise in bed is unexcelled!"

A few days later, the good doctor arrives home to find the entire house darkened. Upon hearing noises on the second floor, he mounts the stairs, goes up to the master bedroom and pounds on the locked door.

"Henrietta? Henrietta! Is that you? Are you in there?"

"Yes, Lionel, I'm here."

"Well, open the door! What's going on, Henrietta?"

"Sorry, Lionel, but I'm in bed with Dr. Lippenzanner from next door."

"What? You're in bed with Lippenzanner? What's going on?"

"Not much, Lionel. I'm just getting a second opinion."

READ AT YOUR OWN RISQUE!

103. MEDICAL SPECIALIST TOWER.

O'Leary requires a tooth extraction. His dentist is located in the renowned Pittsfield Building in downtown Chicago, one of those marvelous towers filled almost exclusively with a wide variety of specialists in the medical and dental profession.

O'Leary is sitting in the dentist's chair, now properly anesthetized. The dentist asks him to open wide, grasps a molar firmly and yanks.

The tooth is extracted – but unfortunately, the tooth extracting instrument slips and the molar rolls down O'Leary's throat. He gags. He chokes. The dentist throws up his hands in consternation. As O'Leary struggles there in the chair, clutching his throat, the dentist exclaims, "Oh, heavens! I'm sorry! I'm terribly sorry, Mr. O'Leary, but don't worry! The problem can be easily solved. You are fortunate to be in a building filled with medical specialists and – lo and behold – there is a throat man right next door. Come!"

With that, the dentist put his arm around O'Leary and leads him out of the office, into the hall, and next door into the office of a noted throat man. The nurses are informed of the crisis and O'Leary is rushed into one of the examination rooms. The throat specialist shines a light down O'Leary's throat and squints carefully through the instrument.

"Oh, damn. We just missed it! If only you had gotten here 30 second sooner! But I'm sorry to say it's beyond my area. It's now descended into your stomach and you need an internist! But no problem! Don't worry! You happen to be in a building filled with medical specialists and there is a marvelous internist just two floors below us. Quick, come! Quickly! I'll take you there!"

The throat man takes O'Leary and leads him into the elevator, they descend two floors and rush down the hall to the internist. Once again, the nurses are quickly informed of the crisis and O'Leary is rushed into the examination room where he confronts one of the city's finest internists. Immediately, he is fluoroscoped. The internist takes the reading carefully. "Ah-hah! Oh my goodness! What a shame! If only you had been brought here one minute sooner, we could have done something for you. I'm sorry, Mr. O'Leary, but the problem is simply out of my territory. It's now down into your intestinal cavity and I absolutely must turn you over to a GI man. Luckily for you, we have one of the world's finest GI men just six floors above us. Come quickly! I'll take you there!"

With that, the internist rushes O'Leary to the elevator, they ascend six floors and O'Leary is rushed down the hall and into the inner sanctum of one of the world's finest gastro-intestinal specialists. Once again, O'Leary is fluoroscoped and once again, the specialist exclaims, "Oh, no! Oh, no! What a pity! If only they had brought you in three minutes sooner. The problem, Mr. O'Leary, is that it is now simply beyond my territory. But lucky you – we have one of the world's most renowned proctologists just seven floors below us. Come quickly, I'll take you there!"

The GI man leads O'Leary down the hall to the elevators and they descend seven floors. He rushes O'Leary into the proctologist's office. The nurses summon the great guru, and they yank O'Leary pants off, put him up on the table with his posterior protruding into the air, and the proctologist jams a probe light into O'Leary's anus.

"Wait a minute! Hold everything!" screams the proctologist. "That's a tooth up there! You need a dentist!"

CHAPTER NINE

PROFESSIONALISM

Expertise Is In The Eye of the Beholden.

104. SOMEBODY'S LION.

A circus loses its lion tamer and posts an audition for new candidates.

On the appointed day, two applicants show up at the big top, which is deserted this afternoon except for the center ring, which contains a cage full of lions. The circus producer greets the two applicants, a very handsome, muscular young man who goes by the stage name of "Boris the Bold" and a stunningly beautiful blonde who bills herself as "Millicent the Magnificent."

After interviewing each and reviewing their respective résumés, the producer says, "Okay, who would like to try out first?"

Gallantly, Boris turns to the blonde and says, "After you, madam."

Without a blink or a smile, the young blonde steps smartly into the cage, marches to the center, cracks her whip and instantly every lion jumps to its perch. She then cracks the whip again and all lions sit up on their hind legs obediently. Finally, she fixes a steely gaze upon the king lion, stabs her forefinger at him, and then crooks her finger, commanding him to leave his perch and crawl to her feet. The king lion does so meekly. The young lady then proceeds to strip completely and stands there nude and statuesque in the center ring. She cracks the whip once again and the king lion stretches out his tongue and begins to lick her entire body from top to bottom and back again. Standing transfixed outside the cage, the producer sucks in his breath, totally blown away by the performance. He shakes his head in disbelief. Finally, he turns to the male applicant standing next to him and asks, "Well, do you think you can do better than that?"

"Can I ever! Just get those fucking lions out of that cage!"

105. MONUMENTAL TRIBUTE.

A tourist group was touring Jerusalem and came upon Israel's Tomb of the Unknown Soldier.

Among the visitors, one woman took notice of the plaque on the monument. It read:

> NATHAN SCHWARTZ
> A GREAT FURRIER
> 5694-5733.

Looking somewhat confused, the woman approached the tour guide. "Sir, may I ask you a question?" He nodded. "How could this be the Tomb of the Unknown Soldier when Israel has clearly identified him on the monument?"

"Madam," says the tour guide, "the inscription is entirely accurate and valid. As a solder, Nathan Schwartz was totally unknown. But as a furrier, he was awesome."

106. DEPARTMENT OF TRANSPORTATION.

At a US Marine Corps base in Kuwait, a brand new Marine captain arrives. During his first inspection of the outfit, he happens to notice a camel hitched up behind the mess tent. "Sergeant," he says, "why the hell is that camel tied up behind this mess tent?"

The sergeant replies nervously, "Well, sir, as you know, there are 500 men on this post and absolutely no women. And sir, sometimes men have certain urges? That's why we have Shirley the camel."

The captain whispers, "Well, I can't say that I really condone this type of thing, but I understand about male urges. So I guess the camel can stay."

About a month later, the captain starts having his own urges and, crazy with passion, he asks the sergeant to bring the camel to his tent. Putting the ladder behind the camel, the captain stands on the ladder, pulls his pants down and has insane sex with the camel.

When he's quite finished, he looks down and asks the sergeant, "Sergeant, tell me, is that how the other men do it?"

"Not really, sir," says the sergeant. "Usually, they just ride the camel into town where the girls are."

107. THE PERFECT PROPOSITION.

A mid-level copywriter in the creative department of a New York ad agency is laying in bed one night when suddenly, Mephistopheles appears at his bedside.

The young man sits up, rubs his eyes in disbelief and stares at the devil, who has now taken a seat on the edge of the bed. Before he can utter a word, the devil says, "This is your lucky day, my friend, your lucky day. I'm here to offer you an incredible bargain. You will agree to give me your soul for all of eternity. In return, I am going to do the following: I'm going to arrange for you to win the General Motors account next week. The following week, you will win the Procter & Gamble account. The week after that, I will see that you personally land the American Airlines account. And the week after that, I'll see that you are awarded the Budweiser account. Three months from now, I will arrange for you to win nine Cleo awards for the sheer genius storyboards that you are creating. Within six months, all of this will lead to your election as Executive Vice President and Creative Director of the agency. You'll have a plush corner office, three secretaries and a $2 million salary. How about that?"

The ad man scratches his head, squints at the devil and says, "Okay …okay…but wait a minute…what's the catch?"

108. SUCCESSION SUCKS.

The CEO of a major corporation is canned by his board of directors. As he is in his office cleaning out his desk, his replacement has already arrived. The new CEO strolls into the office, shakes hands with his predecessor and asks, "George, you've had a tough ride. Could you give me any helpful parting advice? Any eternal words of wisdom?"

The outgoing CEO beams brightly and says, "Not only can I – but I already have, in the form of these three envelopes. I have timely advice for you in each of them and I have numbered them sequentially. Please open each as you feel the need."

In the months following, things continue to go poorly for the hapless corporation and finally, one evening, the new CEO, harried and tired and working late in his shirtsleeves, finally decides that he had best open envelope number one. He removes it from the desk drawer and unseals it, reading the first piece of advice. It said: "CLEAN HOUSE! OVERHAUL ALL SYSTEMS AND PROCEDURES! START FRESH! PUSH YOUR IDEAS BOLDLY!"

A few more months pass and quarterly sales are continuing to plummet while profit margins dwindle to a negligible pittance. In a fit of frustration, the CEO opens his desk draw once again and unseals envelope number two. Its message reads: "RESTRUCTURE! DOWNSIZE! OUTSOURCE!"

A few more months pass and sales continue to erode. The company is now swimming in red ink. Once again, the CEO is burning the midnight oil and, in desperation, yanks open his desk drawer and feverishly grasps the third envelope. He rips it open and reads its message: PREPARE THREE ENVELOPES."

109. OUT OF THE DEPTHS.

Like many husbands, Mr. Finkelstein occasionally forgets and leaves the toilet seat up.

On this particular night, in the wee hours, Mrs. Finkelstein finds the urge and gropes her way through the pitch darkness to the bathroom, where she turns around and settles down, only to find herself totally immersed in the toilet bowl. Try as she might, she cannot extricate herself. Finally, she screams, "Max! Max! You schmuck! Come look what you did! You left the toilet seat up and now I can't get out of here. Get your ass in here and help!"

Aroused from his sleep, Finkelstein staggers into the bathroom and tries vainly to extricate his wife. He tugs, he pulls, he pushes. He tries to yank her straight up and to either side. All to no avail. Her torso remains firmly planted in the bowl.

"Well, you schmuck! Now what are you going to do? Don't just stand there! Get me out of here! Go call a plumber!"

Finkelstein rushes to the Yellow Pages, finds an emergency plumber, dials the number and luckily connects with a service. "Okay, darling, don't panic. They'll be right over. We'll get you out in no time!"

"Finkelstein! I can't believe what a schmuck you are! Don't you realize that I'm sitting here totally nude? What do you expect to do – have the plumber walk in and see me nude like this? Quick, dummy! Quick! Get me something to cover up!"

His nerves jangled, Finkelstein grabs the first thing available – his Yamulka – rushes in to the bathroom and places it over his wife's vaginal area. Just then, the doorbell rings and the speedy plumbing service has arrived. Finkelstein opens the door and ushers the plumber into the bathroom. He then retreats to the bedroom and paces the floor. Five minutes later, the plumber emerges from the bathroom.

"Well?" says Finkelstein, "what's the verdict?"

The plumber frowns and says, "Mr. Finkelstein...I think I can get your wife out of there, but the rabbi's a goner."

110. JACK OF ALL CHORES.

Gina throws up her hands in frustration. "Guido! Guido! Get down here in the kitchen right away!"

Guido saunters downstairs and answers in a tired voice, "What is it, Gina?"

"Guido, the garbage disposal is all screwed up. You're going to have to stop everything and fix it."

Guido stands there and stares at his wife like she has lost her mind. "Gina, are you kidding? Do you see P-L-U-M-B-E-R written across my forehead? I'm not going to touch that damn thing, and I'm busy anyway watching the ballgame. Go call a professional."

Three days later, Gina throws up her hands in frustration. "Guido! Guido! Look at this place! It's a mess! That baseboard is cracked and needs replacing. This molding is coming loose and has to be fixed, and the bathroom door is warped and won't close anymore and needs to be planed on the bottom. Come on, get busy!"

Guido stands there and stares at her. "Gina, are you out of your skull? Do you see the word C-A-R-P-E-N-T-E-R written across my forehead? That's not a job for me. Besides, I'm going out bowling tonight. Go call a professional!"

Three days later, Guido comes home from work to find the entire living room ransacked. He runs into the kitchen and yells, "Gina! Gina! What happened?"

His wife is sitting calmly at the kitchen table. "Well, Guido, I've had quite a day. A burglar broke into the house, held me at gunpoint while he ransacked the place looking for money and jewels. When he didn't find any, he forced me into the kitchen here and said I had two choices. I could either bake him a rich devil's food cake, which he loves, or else give him oral sex."

"So what did you do, Gina?" says Guido.

"Do you see B-E-T-T-Y C-R-O-C-K-E-R written across my forehead?"

111. CHIEF GREETER.

Harry is making his usual call to his aging mother in California.

"Hi, Mom, how are you doing?"

"I'm fine, Harry. Everything's fine here, and guess what? I got a job."

"You got a job? Mother, what in the world do you need a job for?"

"Well, Harry, at my age I decided I still need something to keep me busy, to keep me occupied and to earn a little extra money on the side, so I got a steady job and I'm loving it."

"Well, what's the job, Mother?"

"I'm a receptionist!"

"A receptionist? Where are you a receptionist, Mother?"

"In a sperm bank."

"A sperm bank! What in the world do you do there?"

"It's easy. All I do is sit there and as each man leaves I say, 'Thanks for coming!'"

112. COMPARING NOTES.

Three alluring young ladies of the evening, top professionals in their business, are enjoying a late evening cocktail together, between engagements, in the bar at New York's Four Seasons Hotel. The conversation drifts around to the subject of disagreeable traits possessed by the various common categories of their clientele.

"The professional category I really can't stand," says the first young lady, "are the lawyers. They are so fucking irritating! Invariably, they will engage you, take you up to the hotel room, and spend the first half hour of the session giving you a complete interrogation. I mean, it's like a whole deposition. They want your life history, and they want the whole truth and nothing but the truth."

"Yeah," says the second, "they're pretty aggravating, but the ones I find really exasperating are the doctors. They engage you, take you up to the hotel room and spend the first 40 minutes giving you a complete physical examination. I mean, they want to check you over 100 percent before even touching you. That stuff drives me up the wall!"

"Okay, okay," says the third, "those groups are pretty nauseating. But the ones that I find the most tedious and that really drive me to distraction are the PR men."

"The PR men?"

"Yes, they're the worst. A PR man engages you, takes you up to the room and spends the first 50 minutes of the hour sitting on the edge of the bed, telling you how good it's going to be!"

READ AT YOUR OWN RISQUE!

113. THE FIRST SINAI CAMPAIGN.

Moses is furious. He demands to see his PR counsel immediately.

When the counsel arrives, Moses throws his hands toward the heavens and screams, "Manny, I am really agitated. I mean, I'm really at my wit's end. I'm on the verge of terminating our contract."

"Now, Mose, stay calm," counsels Manny.

"Stay calm? Stay calm? How can I stay calm when I'm getting no coverage? Here I've been paying you fancy retainers to help me let the world know about the plight of the Israelites in Egypt – and I'm getting almost no ink! You and your big ideas! Three weeks ago you had me stand up before the entire court of Pharaoh and wave my hand and burn a bush! That took a lot of doing on my part, and do you know what I got? A one-column picture on the back page of the *Cairo Tribune*! That's crap!"

"But, Mose..."

"Just a minute, Manny! I'm paying you for strategic thinking, and what do you give me? Two weeks ago, you tell me stand up before the Pharaoh's court and hold up my staff and turn it into a fucking snake. Do you know what it takes to do that? Do you? And do you know what it got me? A lousy four column inches on Page 27 of the *Alexandria Times*. You call that coverage?"

"But what about the plague of locusts, Mose?"

"Big deal, Manny. The coverage I got on that one wasn't worth the papyrus that it was printed on!"

"Okay, Mose, Okay, I've got it. Here's one that is guaranteed to give you worldwide visibility. I mean, this will give you worldwide media play with precisely the positive spin that you've been seeking. Just listen to this scenario. Next Friday night, you're going to pack up all of our people, all of them. The preparations will have to be hasty. Don't let them take time to do anything like baking bread. Have them pack up all their belongings, and then in the middle of the night, move them out of Egypt and across the Sinai. When you get to the Red Sea, we'll have the media on-hand. It will be a fantastic media spectacle. You will stand there in your white robe on the shores of the Red Sea, and you will slowly wave your hand. You will part the sea, Mose. Yes, you will wave your hand and roll back the waters and then lead our people across, donkeys, camels and all. Then when the Egyptian army sends its chariots chasing our people and begins to cross the sea, you will stand on the other shore and wave your hand once again and allow the sea to swallow them up! It will be beautiful!"

"Wait a minute, Manny, must wait a minute. You expect me to engineer that entire thing by Friday? That's going to take a hell of a lot of doing! I don't even know if I have all of the powers I can summon up to make it happen! But if I manage to do it, Manny, will it all be worth it?"

Manny grabs Moses by both shoulders and looks him squarely in the eye. "Worth it? Worth it? Mose, if you can pull this off, I will personally – I mean personally – guarantee you at least four full pages in the Old Testament!"

CHAPTER TEN

WEDDINGS

Wipe That Loehengrin Off Your Face.

114. PREMARITAL PRECIPICE.

It's one day prior to his wedding. Sheldon has a problem. A button has popped off of his tuxedo and he needs some seamstress attention. He drives to the house of his bride, Hortense, leaves the car at the curb, walks to the door, knocks and it is opened by none other than Sadie, the younger sister of his bride. No one else is at home.

He explains his plight to Sadie and Sadie is perfectly accommodating. She immediately attaches the button. Then she becomes even more accommodating. "You know, Sheldon, this is your last day of freedom. Perhaps what you don't know, Sheldon, is that I've always had a tremendous yen for you and am awfully jealous of my sister. I'd just love for the two of us to take this one last opportunity to make it with each other before I lose you forever. What do you think?"

Sheldon blushes, shifts nervously and cogitates.

Sensing his indecision, Sadie says, "Sheldon, let me make it easy for you. I'm going to go upstairs right now to my bedroom and I'm going to strip naked. If you'd like one last fling, just come upstairs in the next five minutes." With that, she waltzes up the stairway.

Sheldon thinks for a moment, gets up, walks quickly across the foyer, opens the front door and heads for his car. Suddenly, to his amazement, he sees the family SUV in the driveway and the entire remainder of the bride's family is sitting there, including the bride herself.

His father-in-law-to-be leans out the window of the SUV, waves both hands, and says, "Hooray for you, Sheldon!" followed by a tremendous round of applause by the entire family in the van. "This was your final test before your wedding, and you passed with flying colors. Congratulations, my new son!"

Sheldon smiles, waves both arms in the air and accepts the ovation with great poise and equanimity.

The moral of the story: Always, always keep your condoms in your car.

115. EXCHANGE OF VOWS.

The groom is walking slowly down the aisle. He has an enormous grin on his face. He is the picture of elation. Finally, he gets to the altar and takes his position next to the best man.

"Wow, George," says the best man, "are you ever on a high! I've never seen you so overjoyed!"

"Well, Fred, I have to tell you, confidentially, that I just had the greatest blow job of my life," whispers the groom.

Suddenly, the trio of piano, violin and viola begin the processional. On her father's arm, the bride begins the slow march down the aisle, beaming with freshness and radiance. She is grinning from ear-to-ear.

When she arrives at the altar, her maid of honor whispers, "Hey, honey, what's up? I mean, I know this is your wedding and all that, but, like, you look as if you're about to explode with happiness. I know this is a blessed event, but aren't you overdoing it?"

"You don't understand," whispers the bride, "I just gave the last blow job of my life!"

116. NASAL EXTENSION.

Pinocchio and his wife leave the wedding and head for their honeymoon hotel. Once in the room, they pour some champagne, tear their clothes off and hop into bed.

In a frenzy of passion, Mrs. Pinocchio jumps in bed, rolls him over on his back and says, "Okay, this is what I've been waiting for! I'm going to sit on your face and I want you to lie to me! Lie to me! Lie to me!"

117. POST-MARITAL BLISS.

The bride walks down the aisle with her father. They kiss. She proceeds to the altar and joins her groom. As the music stops and the minister is about to begin the ceremony, she happens to notice out of the corner of her eye a set of golf clubs standing next to the groom. She pokes him with her elbow and whispers, "Honey, aren't those your golf clubs standing there?"

"Yes, dear, they are," says the groom.

"Well, what on Earth are they doing here?"

"Well, this isn't gonna' take all day, is it?"

Ted Pincus

118. NUTRITIONAL HAZARDS.

In an evening lecture series at a nursing home, a noted nutritional authority is at the lectern. He asks the group, "Who among you can tell me what food would be considered the most harmful to the human body?"

A lady in the first row raises her hand and says, "That's easy. It's well-marbled sirloin steak, with all that horrendous cholesterol."

An elderly gentleman in the second row raises his hand and says, "I think it's rich chocolate mousse, with all that terrible sugar content!"

Another lady in the same row raises her hand and says, "I'd like to nominate duck liver, with all of those poisons it contains!"

"Is there anyone else who can tell me what food on this planet causes the most grief and suffering?" says the lecturer.

In the last row, Mrs. Rednick raises her hand, rises to her feet and yells out, "Vedding cake!"

119. THE MATCHMAKER.

In a tiny shtetl, not far from Minsk, just a century ago, there lived a middle-aged matchmaker name Yetta. She wasn't living very well, however, because business was lousy. Her matches just weren't matching up very well and that meant that fee volume was pretty slim.

Undaunted, however, Yetta sits back and stretches her imagination. Creativity was the name of the game in matchmaking. And today, as she sits there staring at her dingy office wall, the latest brainstorm captivates her fertile mind. Out of her chair she leaps, grabs her cape and her bonnet and streaks down the muddy street to burst in upon Yitzak, the tailor's son.

"Yitzak, my friend! This is your lucky day! Yetta has new merchandise! Have I got a woman for you!"

"Oy, come on, Yetta," the handsome, strapping young lad replies. "Not again! You know very well that if I were ever going to marry anybody, I'd marry Zelda, the shoemaker's daughter!"

"I know, I know! But Yitzak! Wait a minute! You've gotta' hear this one! This is a master stroke! It's too good to pass up! This is the woman of your dreams!"

"Oh, yeah? I don't believe it. What is this woman of my dreams all about, Yetta?"

"She fantastic, Yitzak, fantastic! First of all, she's gorgeous. She has skin and teeth as white as the driven snow. She has beautiful flaxen hair that rolls in ringlets down her back. She has ruby red lips and aquamarine eyes and a figure that's right out of a fairy tale. Her bustline is supple and uplifted and yet voluptuous. Her waist is tiny. Her hips are incredibly curvaceous. But that's just for openers, Yitzak. She's also brilliant. What a mind! Fabulously intelligent and cultured. And that's not all, Yitzak, here's the best part. She's got millions, yes, millions of rubles. She's absolutely loaded. It's an ideal match for you, Yitzak!"

The young lad hunched over his needle and thread and continued stitching. "Well, I don't know, Yetta. I don't know. I think I still have my heart set on Zelda. Sorry, but nice try."

The Matchmaker leaves in despair, but not in defeat. A week later, she is back again, regaling Yitzak, the tailor's son, with ever more vivid descriptions of the woman of his dreams. But again, to no avail. A week later, she is back again. And a week after that, and a week after that, she persists. In fact, every week for seven months, Yetta persists in her marketing efforts, embellishing the description with more vivid details each time.

Then one morning, it happens. Yitzak's will is broken. "Okay, Yetta," he says wearily, peering up at her beaming face from the damaged fly he is mending. "You win, you win. She just sounds too enticing. I'll do it. I'll take the match. Tell me who it is and make the arrangements. Go tell her father and let's get the process started. Who is this woman of my dreams?"

"The Czar's daughter."

"The Czar's daughter? The Czar's daughter? Yetta, you're matching me up with the daughter of the Czar?"

"Yes!"

"Well, Yetta, I'm speechless. This is too amazing for words! I mean…I guess…well, okay…you've got a deal!"

The woman arose in an explosion of relief. "Oy, thank God! That's half the battle over with!"

120. FISHING EXPEDITION.

It is the late 1940s when the transatlantic passengers flew propeller-driven planes. Mr. and Mrs. Tietelbaum are standing on the tarmac at the old Idlewild Airport on Long Island, anxiously awaiting the arrival of their daughter Zelda, who has spent several months in Africa doing post-graduate work.

The Tietelbaums' hearts skip a beat as they see the four-engine TWA plane approaching and landing at the field. It taxis over to the gate, comes to a stop, the door opens and the stairway is rolled up and placed into position.

Lo and behold, Zelda is one of the first passengers to appear in the doorway. She is arm-in-arm with an eight-foot tall Watusi, clad in a lion skin, his hair braided, a bone protruding through his nose, a giant green gourd in his right hand, and a writhing snake in his left.

As the couple descend the stairway together, a very agitated Mrs. Tietelbaum cups her hands and yells, "No, no, Zelda! We said bring back a RICH doctor!"

121. RULES OF ROMANCE.

A young man and his bride-to-be pay a visit to their Hasidic rabbi in Brooklyn to get some advice in advance of their wedding.

"Tell us, Rabbi," says the young man, "what are the laws about sex that we must observe once we are married?"

"Vell," says the old rabbi, stroking his gray beard, "da main ting you have to remember after you are married is that dere must be NO DENCING! Remember, no dencing!"

"Rabbi, what about conventional intercourse in bed with the man on top?" says the young bride-to-be.

"Intercourse?" says the rabbi. "No problem. No problem at all. Intercourse leads to babies and propagates our people. Dat's good."

"Well, Rabbi," says the young man, "what about oral sex?"

"Oral sex?" says the rabbi. "Oral sex? No problem. Dat's good, because it leads to intercourse which leads to propagation of our people."

"And Rabbi, what about anal sex?" asks the young bride-to-be.

"Anal sex, hmmmn," muses the rabbi. "Yes. Yes, I suppose the laws permit that, because that could lead to conventional intercourse which could lead to babies and propagate our people. No problem."

"Rabbi, what about having intercourse while standing up in the shower?" asks the young man.

"Standing up it the shower?" exclaims the rabbi. "Absolutely not! That could lead to dencing!"

CHAPTER ELEVEN

MARRIAGE

Two's A Crowd.

122. THE DEVIL, YOU SAY

A man leaves his friends at an encampment in Utah's Monument Valley. He wanders out into the moonlit night. As he enters an eerie canyon, he feels the presence of an evil atmosphere. Some compulsion forces him to wander further. As he rounds a bend in the canyon, there, on a rock, not more than 30 feet from him, stands none other than Mephistopheles.

The devil raises his hands on high, assumes a threatening stance, and yells, "Eeeeyaa!"

The human being stands there motionless, speechless and stupefied.

Once again, the devil raises his hands and yells even louder, "Eeeeyaa!"

This time, the man simply widens his stance, folds his arms across his chest and gives the devil a rather bored, skeptical look.

"Hey, wait a minute, buddy," says the devil, "don't you know who I am?"

"Yes, of course I do."

"Then why the hell aren't you terrified? Don't you realize that I could fry you to a fucking crisp with one lightning bolt out of my hand?"

"Yes, I do."

"And don't you realize that with my other hand, I could cast a spell over you that would turn you into stone for an eternity?"

"Yes, I do."

"And do you understand that I could condemn you to rot in hell for the rest of your days?"

"Yes, I do."

"Then, why the hell aren't you terrified shitless?" screams the devil.

"Because for the past 37 years, I've been married to your sister."

123. THE LAYAWAY PLAN.

On her wedding night, Matilda informs her husband, George, that prior to making love, he will be required to place a $20 bill on the dresser for her.

"Moreover, George," she continues, "my requirement is that you will pay that price each time we make love, for the rest of our lives. Am I not worth it?"

Seeing this as a novel twist on a marital relationship, George decides to humor his bride and readily consents. He places the initial $20 bill on the dresser, and throughout the rest of their marriage, he continues this ritual.

It is now 32 years later, and George is standing there in the bedroom in deep despair. Over recent years, his business has increasingly deteriorated and now is almost on the rocks. The family is deeply in debt and has little cash. In frantic desperation, he walks over to the wall and begins smashing his head against it, crying out in anguish.

"George! George! Don't be so despondent. It isn't that bad!" says his wife.

"Oh, yes, it is! We're in poverty, all is lost!"

Matilda smiles and takes his arm tenderly, motioning him toward the window. "Wait, George, I've got news for you. Wonderful news. Here, take a look out the window. You see that bank at the corner? Do you know what? We own 90 percent of the stock in that bank! Yes, George, you and I. I never told you that all these years, the $20 that you pay me each time we make love has been invested in the stock of that bank. Quietly, it has built up a major sum. Today, we are the majority owners and control the board. And this year, it will begin paying huge dividends. We're rich, George! You can relax!"

George stands there for a moment incredulous. He stares at her, then grimaces, turns around and returns to the wall and begins smashing his head against it once again.

"George! Didn't you hear me? I said we're rich, George! We're rich!"

"You don't understand!" says George, as he continues smashing his head. "I'm such an idiot! If I had only known what a savvy investor you were, I would have given you ALL my business!"

124. THE APHRODESIAC.

Seymour Greenebaum and his wife, Yolanda, have been married over 40 years. Their lovemaking has become a bit stale. Being contemporary and enlightened, they jointly elect to see a sex therapist.

Midway through their first session, the therapist has identified the problem. It seems Mrs. Greenebaum is having great difficulty experiencing an orgasm nowadays.

"Mrs. and Mrs. Greenebaum, I think I have the solution for you. It's an unconventional one, but I've found that it is a formula that has a significant success rate. Here's what I want you to do. When you go home today, I want you to engage the services of a young, good-looking assistant. Tomorrow night, have that assistant come to your apartment and join you in the bedroom. I want the two of you to strip naked as usual, and for Mr. Greenebaum to mount Mrs. Greenebaum in bed in the usual manner. I then want you to instruct your assistant to take a large bath towel and wave it over both of you violently as you make love. If he does it properly, I can predict that Mrs. Greenebaum will get off with no problem."

Dubious but desperate, the couple goes home, engages the services of a husky young good-looking doorman at their building, and makes an appointment for the following evening. That evening, in conformity to the therapist's plan, they equip the young man with a large bath towel and they proceed to make love in bed while he waves it over them.

The next day, they are back for a second session with the therapist. "Well, folks, how did it go?" asks the therapist.

"Well, I must confess that nothing happened," says Mrs. Greenebaum. "It was the same as usual. No success."

The therapist ponders for a moment, then his face brightens and he says, "Okay, I see. Well, I have an alternative plan that I can almost guarantee for success. Here's what I want you to do. Tonight, I want you to engage the same young man, bring him up to your bedroom, get undressed and re-enact the same scene, except have the young man mount Mrs. Greenebaum in bed while you, Mr. Greenebaum, will wave that towel over them as furiously as you can."

The couple looks at each other skeptically, but agree to give it a try.

That evening, the young doorman is hired once again, brought to the bedroom, all three participants undress, Mrs. Greenebaum assumes her position in bed and is mounted by the young man. Meanwhile, Mr. Greenebaum mans the towel and begins to wave it energetically over the rhythmically undulating bodies of the couple in bed. Passion mounts. Within two minutes, Mrs. Greenebaum is screaming in ecstasy and gasping in a paroxym of joy. She is seeing stars. Finally, as the couple lay there motionless and exhausted, Mr. Greenebaum smiles triumphantly, leans over and says to the young doorman, "Now then, you see? THAT'S the way to wave a towel!"

125. KEPT IN THE DARK.

Beginning with their wedding night, Sophie always insisted that they only make love in the dark – no lights whatsoever. Sidney had no problem agreeing to this restriction. Without any variance, this practice is maintained over the years.

They've now been married 35 years. One night, Sophie has a complete change of mind. Burning with a bizarre curiosity, one night in the midst of lovemaking, she reaches over to the bed light and snaps it on. To her total shock, she discovers that Sidney is not penetrating her whatsoever, but instead has inserted a long white plastic dildo.

"Sidney! Sidney! What on Earth? Is that what I think it is?"

"Yes, dear, it is," says her husband sheepishly. "It's a marital aid."

"And have you been using that regularly?"

"Yes, I have."

"You mean…for years?"

"Yes, dear, for years."

"Are you telling me that you've been using that exclusively throughout our entire marriage?"

"Yes, I have."

"Well, Sidney, that's shocking! You'd better explain this!"

"Okay, dear, I will. But first, you explain the kids."

126. EROTIC LUBE.

Rostand, Lenzini and Rabinowitz meet in a Paris bar. After an hour of getting acquainted and after several cocktails, their conversation turns to their sex lives.

"Mon amis," says the Frenchman, "let me describe for you my technique for making love. First, I strip my wife naked very gently, zen I cover her entire body with Beurre Blanc. Zen I put her gently in bed and we make mad, passionate love. It leaves her screaming for ten minutes."

"That's a-very nice," says the Italian, "but the way I make a-love is to rip-a my wife's clothes off, cover her entire nude-a body with olive oil, throw her on the mattress and then make-a mad, passionate a-love. This leaves her screaming for an hour."

"And what about you, Rabinowitz?"

"Vell," says Rabinowitz, "I very politely ask my wife's permission to remove her clothing, then I cover her entire naked body mit schmaltz. Then we make crazy love. Afterwards, she's screaming for three hours."

"Three hours! How could that be?" his two companions ask in unison.

Rabinowitz replies, "That's after I wipe my hands on the drapes."

127. RULES TO LIVE BY.

The sons are gathered around the fireplace, listening to the family patriarch. They are eager for his wisdom. They ask him to give them a lifetime lesson. What are the most important axioms?

"My sons, in my view there are four critically vital rules of a successful life: first, find a woman who is a nymphomaniac in bed. Second, find a woman who is immensely loaded with inherited funds. Third, find a woman who is an accomplished gourmet cook."

"And what is the fourth rule, Papa?" the sons ask.

"Never allow these three women to ever meet."

128. MISCUE ALA CARTE.

A middle-aged man is in the supermarket and in too much of a hurry. As he careens down the aisle and round the corner, he bumps into an attractive young woman. The carts collide.

"Oops, sorry," he exclaims. "Wait a minute. Don't I know you?"

"Of course," says the young woman. "I have one of your kids."

The man is stunned, flustered and stammering. "Oh, my God! Are you the one? Are you the one that I layed on the pool table at my bachelor party when I was blind drunk?"

"No," she replied. "I'm your son's math teacher."

129. THE OPPORTUNIST.

A husband walks into the bedroom to see his wife packing her suitcases.

"Where are you going, honey? On a trip?"

"Yes, I'm leaving for New York. I understand prostitutes there get $400 an hour for what I do for free here."

The husband immediately races to the closet and begins packing his own suitcases.

"Hey, where are you going?" says the wife.

"I'm going to New York with you, honey. I wanna' see you live on $800 a year."

130. MOISHE THE LEGEND.

A very dapper well-tailored, good-looking middle-aged man hops into a cab on Park Avenue in New York. He asks to be taken to LaGuardia Airport. At the first stoplight, the cab driver turns around in his seat and says, "If you would pardon me, sir, you greatly remind me of a man named Moishe."

"Oh, really?" asks the passenger. "Why is that?"

"Well, it's just everything about you that seems to reflect the same kind of panache that was Moishe's reputation. Moishe was always the best-dressed man on the boulevard. He was the essence of sophistication. He was élan personified. He was a world-traveler, he was a raconteur, he had an IQ in the stratosphere. His mind was a virtual encyclopedia. He was a discriminating gourmet, he was an expert bridge player, he was a superb golfer and was devastating on the tennis court. And yet, throughout all of this, he was kind, compassionate and forever mindful of his family blessings and responsibilities."

"Wow," says the passenger. "He sounds like an amazingly remarkable renaissance man. How well did you know him?"

"Oh, I never knew him," says the cab driver.

"You never knew him?"

"No, I married his widow."

131. AUDITORY EXAM.

Sam is beginning to think that his wife, Blanche, is becoming a bit hard of hearing. He asks the doctor what would be a subtle way to find out if his suspicions are true. The doctor suggests that he try speaking to her from another room and see if she responds, and if not, come a bit closer and then a bit closer until finally she responds. Sam decides that this will be a good strategy.

That evening, Sam is in the bedroom and Blanche is in the kitchen. He calls, "Honey...what's for dinner?"

He hears no response. He comes down the stairs and tries again from the bottom of the staircase. "Honey...what's for dinner?" Again, he hears no response. He tries the same attempt from the living room, but again, he hears no response. Finally, he enters the kitchen and walks right behind her as she stands before the stove. "Honey...what's for dinner?"

"Schmuck, for the fourth time – brisket!"

132. THE CONFESSIONAL.

Jake is upstairs in his bedroom, dying. His wife, Fran, is by his side.

He opens his eyes and looks into hers.

"Fran, my darling," he mutters, "before I go, I have a confession to make. I want you to know that three years ago, I slept with your cousin."

His wife simply nods compassionately and pats his hand.

"And Fran, my dearest, I have another confession. Two years ago, I slept with your sister."

Fran continues to smile and pats his hand.

"And Fran, my sweetheart, I have a further confession to make. This past year, I slept with your mother."

Fran rises and gently caresses his forehead. "Jake...Jake, just lay back and rest and let the poison do its work."

133. THE SEX OLYMPIAD.

A young husband comes home one evening, excitedly carrying a package. When he and his wife are alone in the bedroom and ready to retire, he proudly begins to unwrap the mystery package.

"Guess what I bought today, honey?" he says.

"What is it?" she asks.

"They've come out with a new Olympic Condom. Isn't that neat? They come in three colors: gold, silver and bronze."

"Isn't that nice?" she responds.

"And which color would you like me to wear tonight?" he asks. "How would you like me to wear gold?"

"No," she says, "I think I'd like you to wear silver, so that you can come in second for a change."

134. HEAVENLY RECRIMINATIONS.

Morris and Bertha live to a ripe old age and then pass away within minutes of each other. Now they're in the reception room in Heaven, and St. Peter is giving them the grand tour.

"Let's start with your living accommodation," St. Peter says. "Have a look at this magnificent villa, complete with heavenly views, an ultra-modern kitchen, self-cleaning everything, your own pool and every other comfort imaginable. Now, let's take a look over here, where you have your own private golf course. There won't be any problem in navigating the course, because you'll have all the energy that you had when you were in your twenties. The course is specially constructed so that you will be shooting par golf every round. You'll be able to sustain your energy because your diet will consist of every single delicacy known to mankind, plus many that aren't. There will be no limit on the quantity and you can feel free to gluttonize every meal. You'll find that we have no doctors' offices or dentists' offices up here, because you'll never have an ailment. No aches and pains and no indigestion. And for entertainment, you'll have only the finest ever produced."

"Wow! What do you think, Morris?" asks Bertha.

"I'm furious!" he says. "I'm livid!"

"But why, Morris?"

"Because if it were not for your fucking bran muffins and bean sprouts and yogurt diets, we could've been up here 20 years ago!"

135. RECRUITMENT OFFICE.

A club member is standing at the urinal in the elegant men's room of the posh Northmoor Country Club north of Chicago. At that moment, somebody else's guest strolls into the men's room and steps up to the adjacent urinal. As the two men are standing there, the guest gasps a sigh of appreciation as he gazes around the room at the expensive marble and exquisite fixtures. "Wow," he exclaims as he stands there facing the urinal wall. "The elegance is amazing! This is quite a place. Very impressive!"

"Think so?" says the member.

"Oh, yes," says the guest. "I think the design, materials and furnishings of this entire club reflect the very latest in workmanship and sophisticated taste."

"Well, gee, if you're that impressed, why don't you apply for membership?" whispers the member.

"Oh, I'd love to," says the guest. "I just bought a house a mile from here last year, but I really couldn't apply. I mean, it wouldn't be proper."

"Why not?"

"Well, you see...I'm not Jewish."

"So what? Why should that make any difference?" says the member. "Half of our members are non-Jews!"

"What? You must be kidding! You must be putting me on" says the guest. "I know where I am! This is Northmoor Country Club! What do you mean half of your members are non-Jews?"

"That's right, they are," says the member. "All of our second wives."

136. ESTATE JEWELRY.

Fran Goldman has suffered a mild heart attack and is now convalescing nicely at home, but somehow convinced that her days are now numbered, she soon begins to make feverish preparations for her eventual demise.

She goes through all of the usual preparations. She calls in her attorneys and creates a living trust. She discusses the family assets with her husband and how they can best transfer assets to the children and future generations with minimal taxes. Then, amid these various preparations, she says to her husband, "You know, Irving, the one thing I never had is my own portrait painted. Before I do, I'd like to leave a portrait of me in your hands."

Even though he feels that all this activity is somewhat premature, this request in particular touches her husband's heart strings and he immediately agrees. He calls in one of the city's finest portrait artists to do an oil painting of Fran. The portrait requires four sittings. On the evening that the artist finally departs, Fran finally allows her best friend Shirley to come into her bedroom and view the finished canvas, standing there in all its glory on the easel. When Shirley enters the room and views the painting, she is both impressed and astounded.

"Hey, that's gorgeous! And it's you, it's you! But wait a minute! What's with all the jewelry, Fran?" exclaims Shirley. " In this painting, you're wearing a necklace with a string of pearls the size of golf balls! And earrings with diamonds right out of Harry Winston! And an emerald brooch like right out of a royal collection! How come he painted you with all kinds of jewelry you don't even own?"

"Well, my darling, those were my instructions. You see, after I'm gone, that next bitch Irv marries, I want her to go crazy turning this house upside-down for the rest of her life trying to find these jewels!"

137. THE ULTIMATE THERAPY.

After angioplasty, followed by two bypasses, Davidoff is now visiting the doctor for a post-surgery examination, accompanied by his wife, Hortense.

After the examination, Davidoff leaves the doctor and sits in the waiting room while Hortense is called in for a private consultation with the cardiologist.

"Mrs. Davidoff," says the doctor, "I'm going to have to speak very frankly to you and give it to you straight. Your husband's condition is very delicate and his chances for survival will depend greatly on whether he is given an extreme amount of tender lover care at home. You must follow this prescription to the letter. Every day, from now on, you must assist him with all of his toilet functions, gently shave him in the mornings, prepare a special breakfast for him which will be served to him in bed, then provide him close companionship and attentiveness throughout the day. Mix him a two-ounce, well-chilled martini before dinner, then prepare him a highly specialized low-fat, salt-free, home-cooked dinner which must also be served to him in bed, then offer him his favorite television shows until about 9 p.m., when you will very gently provide a few minutes of oral sex followed by a loving kiss goodnight. This procedure should be followed every day from now on."

She thanks the doctor and re-enters the waiting room.

"Vell," he asks. "Vat did the doctor say?"

"The doctor said you're gonna' die."

138. ALL IN THE FAMILY.

A very dejected middle-aged man is sitting at a bar for an entire evening, downing drink after drink and becoming a sorrier sight with each passing hour.

Finally, the bartender leans over and says, "Hey, Mac, you look like you have big problems."

"Problems? Do I ever have problems! Three months ago, I found out that my oldest son is gay. A month ago, I found out that my middle son is gay. Last week, I found out that my youngest son is gay."

"Boy, those are tough problems. Doesn't anybody in your family like pussy?"

"Yes. Unfortunately, I just found out this afternoon that my wife does."

139. DOMESTIC TRADEOFF.

Mr. Gimpelman is having a consultation with his urologist.

"Morris," says the doctor, "it's my advice that the best step you could take to improve your sex life would be to let me give you a prosthetic penile implant."

"You really think that's the answer, Doc?"

"Yes, I do. That will be the answer to your problem."

"Hmmmn. Okay, what does that kind of procedure cost?"

"I can give you a great one with a lifetime guarantee for just $18,000," says the doctor.

"Gee, I'm going to have to think about that one," Gimpelman says. "I think I had better go home and check this out with Glenda before I give you a final answer."

Two days later, Gimpelman returns to have another consultation with the doctor. "Well, Morris, what's the verdict?"

"Well, Doc, we talked it over and Glenda decided she'd rather redo the kitchen."

140. PLAN MY EVENING.

"Honey, I've got some terrible news to tell you," the young husband said as he flopped heavily into an armchair upon arriving home from work. "They got the tests back today, and the doctor tells me I've got one day to live!"

"Oh, my God!" says his young yuppie wife. "What are we going to do?"

"What are we going to do? What are we going to do? We're going to make the most of tonight, that's what we're going to do! I'm going to put on my tux, you're going to put on your best formal gown, we're going to go out on the town, we're going to have the finest cuisine, the finest champagne, the finest wines. We're going to dance to the wee hours of the morning, and then I'm going to bring you back here and fuck your brains out until dawn!"

"We're going to do what?" asks his wife. "You've got to be kidding! You expect me to put a formal gown on and go chasing around the city with you all evening, drinking and dancing until the wee hours of the morning and then come back here, and you're going to fuck my brains out all night until dawn? Do you have any idea what kind of commitments I have? Do you know that I'm scheduled for an 8 a.m. breakfast meeting with three of our top clients, followed by a seminar that I have to deliver at noon, followed by a presentation in Cleveland that I have to make tomorrow evening? My God, we should chase around all night and live it up? That's easy for you to say. YOU don't have to get up tomorrow!"

141. ETERNAL GRATITUDE.

Astronaut Neil Armstrong is being interviewed on CBS in a detailed retrospective of his illustrious career, centered of course upon his famed moon walk. During the course of the discussion, the interviewer is breaking some new ground. "Neil, now let's turn to a small footnote to history. In our careful review of CBS footage taken during your famed walk on the moon, our re-examination picked up a brief utterance that had not been detected before. Apparently, after you spoke your immortal words to mankind, you muttered under your breath:'Go for it, Ginsberg…' Isn't that true?"

"Yes, John, I must admit it's true," Armstrong confesses.

"But Neil, what could those words possibly have meant? 'Go for it, Ginsberg…' Please tell our listeners."

"Well, John, the untold story is simply this. During all those long months in Houston when we were preparing for our lunar mission, I would receive every week a telegram from a man name Herman Ginsberg, Brooklyn, New York. Each telegram would say things like, 'Dear Neil: I just can't wait until you make it to the moon!' or a message like, 'Dear Neil: I'm so excited that your lunar mission is now just eight weeks away.' Finally, my curiosity got the better of me and I phone Mr. Ginsberg to ask him why he kept sending me all these telegrams informing me of his mounting excitement, and Ginsberg told me: 'Vell, Commander Armstrong, it's very simple. All these years, my wife Zelda has said to me, 'Morris, you'll get oral sex the day a man walks on the moon!'"

142. SUBTLE SIGNALS.

Max and Zelda have been married for more than 30 years and pride themselves on their instinctive ability to know each other's needs.

Nevertheless, one evening in bed before the lights were turned out, Max leans over to Zelda and says, "You know, darling, at our age I think we should develop an improved system of communicating our sexual needs, and I've been thinking about a code that we could devise that might be far more effective that just operating on basic instincts."

"What kind of code, Max?"

"Well, I thought that maybe from now on, after we turn out the lights, on those nights I want sex, I'll reach over in the dark and yank your left breast once. On those nights that I don't want sex, I'll reach over in the dark and yank on your right breast once."

"Okay, Max, what's my code?"

"Well, Zelda, on those nights that you want sex, you reach over in the dark and you grab my schlong and you yank it once, and…on those nights that you don't want sex, you reach over and you yank it 35 times."

CHAPTER TWELVE

CHILDREN

I Kid You Not!

143. THE PSYCHOLOGY OF GENEALOGY.

An old man was sitting on a park bench. Soon, a young lad saunters up the path and sits down next to him. The boy has high-top gym shoes with laces strewn across the ground, baggy pants, a grungy shirt, pierced ears with earrings, a gold ring through his nose, eyebrows dyed orange and spiked hair. One spike is dyed lavender, another spike is dyed bright green, another spike is dyed yellow, and another spike is dyed shocking pink.

The old man cannot help but stare at the sight of this strange creature to his left. After he stares for a full five minutes without interruption, the young boy turns to him and says, "Hey, mister, what's the matter? What are you staring at? That's very rude!"

"I'm sorry for staring at you, I apologize. But let me tell you that once upon a time, I was a young man your age and I was a very, very wild guy. I lived with no restrictions, I followed my impulses. And one night, I got blind drunk and I fucked a parrot."

"So?" asks the boy.

"So I'm thinking," says the old man, "that you may be my son."

144. PATERNAL STRATEGY.

A father in Chicago is on the phone to his son, an attorney living in Los Angeles. "Son, I have news for you."

"What's that, Dad?"

"Son, this is very hard for me to tell you, but your mother and I are splitting."

"What? Are you serious? Dad, that's outrageous! Now, don't do a thing. Don't do anything irrational! Just stay right there, I'll be on the next plane to Chicago and I'm calling my sister and making sure that she meets me there. Just stay put and keep calm!"

The father hangs up the phone and walks toward the kitchen. "Hey, Martha, guess what? The kids are coming for Thanksgiving and they're paying their own airfare!"

145. HANDICAPPED PARKING.

It is a bygone era when Collins Avenue, Miami Beach, was an endless stream of gleaming white hotels – before the days when they all went condo.

It is the elegant circular driveway of the top-of-the-line hotel – the Fontainebleau.

Into the driveway and up to the front entrance pulls a very long, black Lincoln limo. Two doormen in red coats and brass buttons open the rear door of the limo and out pops a quintessential Jewish mother. She immediately beckons that the doormen reach into the rear seat for her 16-year-old son, whom they carefully and comfortably transport into the lobby. Standing next to the car and watching this proceeding, the hotel's livery director comments to the mother, "I'm so sorry, madam, to see your son's disability. It's really a pity that he has to face life in that fashion."

"No, it isn't," says the mother. "He's a perfectly healthy boy, quite physically fit."

"You mean he can walk?" says the observer?

"Yes, but thanks God, he'll never have to."

146. INFANT FORMULA.

An 18-month-old baby is sitting in his highchair. He suddenly grasps a jar of Gerber's prune baby food, picks it up, and as he hurls it across the room, smashing against the opposite wall, he screams, "I hate this shit!"

His mother is stunned, almost speechless. She turns to him and says, "Mortimer! You just said a word! In fact, you just uttered a complete sentence! That's incredible!"

"Really, Mother?"

"Yes, it's amazing! Mortimer, how long have you been able to speak?"

"Well, actually, Mother, I've been able to speak for the past six months."

"Mortimer! That's the most stupendous thing I've ever heard! Six months? Why haven't you said anything up to now?"

"Because up to now, everything has been okay."

147. THE CAREER PLAN.

Goldwasser's daughter gets married, and the couple has now just returned from the honeymoon. Goldwasser asks his new son-in-law to step into his study for a traditional man-to-man chat.

"Well, Gerson, sit down and make yourself comfortable."

"Thanks, Mr. Goldwasser."

Goldwasser pours them both a drink, lights a cigar and sits down to conduct business. "Gerson, I'm not going to mess around or mince words. Here's what I've decided to do. I have a wonderful manufacturing business that's been very good to me. Now that you've married my only daughter, I want to give you a wedding present that will last for life. Right here tonight, I am making you a partner in my business. In fact, here is a certificate signifying that you now own a substantial portion of the equity."

The young man is stunned. For a moment, he is speechless. Finally he says, "Gee, Mr. Goldwasser, I mean, Dad...I just don't know what to say. I just don't know how to thank you."

"No need for thanks, my son. I'm delighted to be able to do it. Now, let's get down to business. Let's have a look at your career. Where would you like to start? How about Shipping? Starting to work in Shipping, you could learn the business from the ground up. You'll see what come in, what goes out. It's the best way to see what it's all about. What do you think?"

"Boy, Dad, that sounds like a wonderful opportunity. I'd really like that. But I have to warn you, I have horrendous asthma and hay fever. I think that if I started in Shipping, with all the dust and fumes, I probably wouldn't last a week."

"Okay, okay, Gerson, no problem. We'll start you in Accounting. That's a wonderful place to start the business. You'll see where the money comes from, where it goes. You'll see what makes the business ticks every day. It'll be marvelous. What do you think?"

"Gee, Dad, that sounds like a terrific opportunity. Accounting would be a very prestigious way to start. But I have to warn you, math was my worst suit, I mean, really. I can't even add two and two. I think I'd make a mess of things within a couple of weeks."

"All right, Gerson, that's no problem. I'll tell you what. Let's start you out in Marketing. We'll put you out on the road. You'll look the client in the face, eyeball to eyeball. You'll hear what he has to say about the product. You'll learn the business that way. It'll be a sensational way to gain some insights into our industry."

"Dad, that's just marvelous and so generous. I really thank you for that chance, and I think I can do very well at it. But I do think you should consider one downside. Remember, I just married your daughter. Our marriage has just begun. If you put me out on the road three, four, five nights a week, there's a chance that maybe our marriage could be on the rocks within six months."

"Okay, Gerson," Goldwasser says with a squint, "then what would you like?"

The two sit silently in the study for many minutes as the grandfather clock ticks away, its pendulum swinging ponderously. Finally, the young man speaks. "Dad, I've been thinking. Now that I'm your partner…why don't you buy me out?"

148. PROPHETABILITY.

Mr. Feldman's daughter, Shirley, has become engaged to a nice young man. One evening early in their engagement period, he's invited to the Feldman's for dinner.

After a pleasant meal and the usual small talk, Mr. Feldman asks Yitzak, the young fiancé, to step into the study for a cigar and a chat.

Once the two men have poured a drink and sat down together, Mr. Feldman says, "Well, Yitzak, tell me what you do for a living."

"Well, Mr. Feldman, I'm a Hasidic scholar. I'm making a lifelong study of the Torah and the Talmud."

"Oh, I see," says Mr. Feldman, "and tell me, once you and Shirley are married, what are your plans for providing income that can put food on the table?"

"Well, sir, I have very steadfast beliefs. I have tremendous faith that God will provide."

"Hmmmnnn. I see. Well, where do you think the money will come to pay the rent and buy clothes for Shirley?"

"Sir, I'm absolutely convinced that God will provide."

"Is that so," says Feldman. "Well, what about when babies arrive and have to be fed and clothed and sent to college? Where are those funds coming from?"

"Mr. Feldman, I have the unshakable conviction that God will provide."

Later that evening after the young man had departed and Feldman was preparing for bed, his wife asked, "How did your discussion go with Yitzak?"

"Well, I must say that, among our four daughters, this is the first time I'm going to have a son-in-law who thinks I'm God."

149. HEAVEN ON SEVEN.

Seymour and Abe are both CEOs of their respective apparel companies on New York's 7th Avenue. Tonight they are commiserating together in a bar on 34th, near 7th, pouring out their problems.

"My biggest problem is a real killer, Abe," says Seymour with tears in his eyes. "You know my son Myron. I put him through the best private schools. I gave him a BMW. I sent him through Yale. I gave him the finest of everything. Then I brought him into the business. I made him a vice president, and you know what I find? Every afternoon he's spending hours in the back room, fucking the models. Oy, what am I going to do?"

"You think you've got problems, Seymour? Ha! That's nothing. I sent my son Herman through Andover and the finest summer camps and then through Harvard and then Harvard Business School, and I gave him a Mercedes and everything he could possibly want, and then I brought him into the business and made him a vice president. And you know what? He spends all afternoon every day in the back room, fucking all the models!"

"So nu, Abe, what's the difference between your problem and mine?"

"You forget, Seymour, I'm in menswear."

150. MY IDEAL.

Once a year, David takes his grandmother out for dinner. She's a little bit hard of hearing, so sometimes he has to embellish his conversation with some meaningful sign language.

Tonight, the two of them are sitting down to dine at a restaurant after many months of absence from each other. After some preliminary pleasantries, David breaks the big news: "Grandma, guess what? I found a girl and I'm getting engaged."

"Oy, dat's vunderful, my David! How marvelous!"

"Yes, Grandma, and we're setting a wedding date for December!"

"Oy, David, you always had a great eye for girls. I'll bet this one is a real vinner! I'm so excited for you. Please describe her to me!"

"Well, Grandma, first, she really has…" (David takes his hands and flutters them down each side of his head to indicate flowing locks and great beauty). The grandmother nods knowingly.

"And also, Grandma, she has…" (David tapes a finger on his right temple, indicating great smarts). The grandmother nods appreciatively.

"And Grandma, she also has plenty of…" (David extends his hand and rubs two fingers together slowly, indicating wealth). The grandmother grins sagely.

"And finally, Grandma, she really has…" (David cups both hands and holds each palm five inches from chest and moves each in a lively tremor, indicating prodigious mammary glands). With that, the grandmother wrinkles her brow and contorts her face.

"Vait a minute, David, vait a minute! I understand that, of course, you would choose a girl with great beauty. And I understand that you would select a young lady with lots of seichel. And it's vunderful that you would pick a girl with lots of gelt. But why, David, why on Earth would you pick a girl with arthritis?"

151. NOMENCLATURE CULTURE.

A young Indian boy is sitting in his teepee, out on the great prairie. Suddenly he turns to his father, the tribal chief, and asks, "Dad, how did I get my name?"

"Well, my son," drones the chief, placing a hand on his little son's shoulder, "in our tribe we have a long-standing tradition. Whenever brave leaves teepee after squaw just give birth to papoose, whatever is first sight that brave beholds upon stepping outside, that is chosen as name for papoose."

"Therefore, my son," the chief continues, "when your brother Running Deer, was born, his mother, the squaw, gave birth to him in the dawn's early light and when I emerged from teepee, the first sight I beheld was a beautiful buck running across the meadow. The same thing with your sister, Soaring Eagle. When your mother, the squaw, gave birth to her, it was beautiful moonlit evening, and as I walked out of teepee, the first sight was a graceful eagle swooping toward heavens. The same thing happened in the naming of your little brother, Swimming Beaver."

The chief smiles down at his son affectionately and places his arm around the little boy's shoulder. "Now do you understand, Two Dogs Fucking?"

152. THE TEXAN.

A Texan is drinking in a New York bar when he gets a call on his cell phone. He hangs up, grinning from ear-to-ear, and orders a round of drinks for everybody in the bar because, he announces, his wife has just produced a typical Texas baby boy weighing 25 pounds.

Nobody can believe that any new baby can weigh in at 25 pounds, but the Texan just shrugs. "That's about average down home, folks. Like I said, my boy's a typical Texas baby boy."

Congratulations are showered on him from all around, and many exclamations of "Wow!" are heard. One woman actually faints due to sympathy pains.

Two weeks later, he returns to the bar. The bartender says, "Say, you're the father of that typical Texas baby that weighed 25 pounds at birth. Everybody's been makin' bets on how big he'd be in two weeks. We were gonna' call you. So…how much does he weigh now?"

The proud father answers, "Seventeen pounds."

The bartender is puzzled and concerned. "What happened? He already weighed 25 pounds the day he was born."

The Texas father takes a slow swig from his longneck Lone Star beer, wipes his lips on his shirt sleeve, leans into the bartender and proudly says, "Had him circumcised."

CHAPTER THIRTEEN

THE CLERGY

Torah! Torah! Torah! And Crucifixations.

153. RAT-TAT-TAT.

The proverbial priest, minister and rabbi are sitting around one day, lamenting an invasion of rats that have been infesting their respective sanctuaries. They are comparing notes on methodology of eradicating the little vermin.

"Well," says the priest, "I've found about 30 percent effectiveness from a new brand of Jarlsberg cheese that we have mounted in traps. It's definitely more effective than the American cheese we've been using."

"Well, gentlemen, we've found an actual better mousetrap," exclaims the minister. "The little bastards hardly have a chance. It has been tremendously effective, and I would estimate that we have eradicated 75 percent of our rodents."

The two then turn to the rabbi for his report.

"Vell...gentlemen...I'm happy to report that we have successfully eradicated 100 percent of our rodent population."

The priest and the minister are stunned. "Gee," says the priest, "that's absolutely amazing! Rabbi, please tell us – by what remarkable technique did you accomplish this?"

"Vell, here vas my strategy: I enlisted the services of several of the young boys of our congregation, and together we scoured the temple for rats and herded them down into the basement. Once we had them locked in the basement, I produced dozens and dozens of tiny talises and yarmulkes which I had ordered in advance from a special tailor friend of mine. I then dressed each rat in a talis and yarmulke. I then bar mitzvah'd each of them, and since that day, my friends, not one of those rats has ever returned to the temple."

154. DISCREET INQUIRY.

The rabbi picks up the telephone. "Hello?"
"Good morning, Rabbi. This is Agent Hector Smith of the Internal Revenue Service."
"Yes, sir? What can I do for you?"
"Do you know a man named Isadore Kohn?"
"Yes, I do."
"Is he a member of your congregation?"
"He is."
"And Rabbi, does he make contributions to your synagogue?"
"He does."
"And did he contribute $10,000 to the synagogue this year?"
"He will."

155. TRADITION IS EVERYTHING.

The congregation is in an uproar. Opinions are split virtually down the middle. Half of the congregation fervently believes that when a service calls for The Shema to be recited, the entire congregation should rise and remain standing throughout the prayer. The other half of the constituents violently disagree and believe that standing is nonsense and that everyone should keep his seat during that sacred prayer. Each side steadfastly believes that tradition supports its belief. The arguments become louder and louder, more and more emotional, and with greater complexity. The situation becomes so intense and acrimonious that the spokesmen from each side finally agree that the only way the debate will be resolved is to go and consult with the eldest member of the congregation, who might very well shed light on a matter of tradition.

Thus, they go to the home of 96-year-old Herschel Bloomberg, who had been a charter member of the congregation.

"Mr. Bloomberg, we desperately need your help," both men plea. "A vicious debate is raging within our congregation. The arguments are endless. About half of the congregants firmly believe and argue for the practice of rising and standing during the recitation of The Shema. The other half are arguing constantly that tradition supports the idea that everyone remain seated. Please, Mr. Bloomberg, tell us which practice is the tradition?"

"Neither," says Bloomberg.

"Neither one? Then tell us, please, what's the tradition?"

"It's the argument. That, my friends, is the tradition."

156. A KNIGHT TO REMEMBER.

Tietelbaum hits the big time as a British industrialist. He has lavish office in Mayfair, country estates in Surrey and Kent, and a fleet of Rolls Royces to transport him between. In fact, Tietelbaum has acquired all that his heart could desire, other than true status in British society.

At last that comes, too. One day he receives, on engraved Buckingham Palace stationery, the official notification from the queen that he has been selected as one of ten of Britain's outstanding businessmen to be knighted that very next April, at ceremonies to be held in Westminster Abbey. He is further informed that he will be hearing shortly from the queen's personal chief of protocol with regard to the required dress for the ceremony and the details of his personal participation.

Bursting with excitement, Tietelbaum anxiously awaits the call from the protocol office. Finally, one day in December, an official from that office calls upon him and explains the proceedings. Essentially, Tietelbaum is told that he must appear in white tie and tails on the appointed date at 10 a.m. at Westminster, participate in the processional, await his turn and then approach the queen, kneel and then recite one brief Latin phrase before receiving his knighthood. He is given the Latin phrase to commit to memory for the occasion.

Coincidentally, the ceremonial date falls precisely on Passover. Being a member of one of London's ultra-reformed congregations, Tietelbaum is undeterred by this coincidence. For weeks in advance of the date, Tietelbaum every evening is practicing recitation of his Latin phrase. His anticipation mounts.

Finally the day arrives. Tietelbaum and his family are driven to Westminster. He takes his place among the nine other candidates, resplendent in their white ties and tails. The trumpets blare, the processional begins, and now each candidate in turn is called upon to walk up the red carpeted aisle and kneel before the queen to receive the honor. Tietelbaum is the last one do to so.

On shaky legs, he walks up the aisle, reaches the throne, kneels before his queen and is about to utter the well-rehearsed Latin phrase. Suddenly he clutches! His mind is blank! Mentally he gropes feverishly for the elusive words, but they just don't come. Finally, after a few moments of total panic and desperation, he utters the one phrase that flows most naturally on that very holiday. He blurts out, "Manish tahna halailah hazehd!"

Cocking her head at him quizzically, the queen leans over and asks the minister at her side, "What makes this knight different than all other knights?"

157. INCOGNITO ENCOUNTER.

President George Bush is sitting at his desk in the Oval Office. He is fuming mad. Standing before him is the Head of the CIA, the Head of the National Security Council and the Chairman of the Joint Chiefs of Staff.

"Why!" Bush screams at the threesome. "Why am I always the last to know? No matter what happens around the globe, why is it that the first ones to find out are the Mossad, and then all the Jews in Israel? And then all the Jews in the US? And then finally, the CIA finds out and tells me! You dummies! I'm tired of this bumbling!"

"We are sorry, sir, we are really trying..." comes the response.

"Well, that's not good enough, gentlemen. There must be some secret to their system, and I'm going to find out what it is! There must be a reason why they learn all the news before I do!"

Bush then proceeds to issue instructions to his resources. He summons the greatest disguise expert in the CIA. He has the specialist transform him into the perfect likeness of a Hasidic Jew. The makeup artist gives Bush a complete transformation with beard, moustache, black coat, black hat – the works. Then, that evening – a Friday – Bush is driven by a plainclothesman CIA agent in an unmarked car to a little Orthodox congregation in Silver Springs, Maryland, and Bush attends the traditional Friday night Sabbath services. Once the service is over, Bush emerges in the outer lobby of the temple to participate in the traditional Oneg Shabat social gathering. He fondles a plastic glass half full of white wine and proceeds to mingle with the crowd of congregants. Spying a very wise-looking elderly man, Bush approaches him, smiles broadly and says, "Good evening!"

"Good evening," says the old man.

Bush's eyes shift suspiciously from side to side and finally are transfixed once again on the old man. He smiles again and says, "So... what's the news?"

"Vat's the news? Haven't you heard?" The old man whispers hoarsely into Bush's ear, "The president's here!"

158. SHULE DAYS – GOLDEN RULE DAYS.

Bernstein and Gelderman were boyhood chums but haven't seen each other in many years. During the intervening decades, Bernstein sank deeper and deeper into abject poverty, while Gelderman hit the big time and now drives around town in a Rolls Royce Silver Cloud.

It just so happens that on this particular day, Gelderman has taken an alternate route through a poverty-stricken ward, halts at a stop light momentarily and glances at the gutter, only to spot his boyhood chum. He can't believe his eyes. Excitedly, he presses the button to lower his electric window, pokes out his head and yells, "Bernstein? Bernstein, is that you?"

From his seat on the curb, Bernstein, clad in the gruesome rags, looks up incredulously, squints at the big sedan and tries vainly to figure out from whom and for what he has been summoned. Suddenly the dawn of recognition comes over him, his face brightens and he screams, "Gelderman! Oh, my God, it's you, Gelderman."

With that, his friend puts on his flasher lights, leaps out of the car, runs over and sits down on the curb next to Bernstein, hugging him with passion. "Bernstein! Bernstein! After all of these years! How wonderful to see you! But…look at you. Just look at you. What on Earth has happened to you?"

Bernstein then regaled Gelderman with two hours of profligacy, imprudent decisions and just plain bad luck. He has lost his business, his house, his wife and almost all worldly possessions. In fact, he is down to his last $60.

"But enough about me, Gelderman," Bernstein says at last. "Enough about me. How about you? Look at you with this fancy car and Savile Row three-piece suit. It sure looks like you're in the chips. How did you make it?"

Gelderman hunches over a bit, looks both ways to be sure he isn't being overheard, and whispers to his friend, "You probably won't believe this, Bernstein, but it's true. I've won millions at the racetrack."

"The racetrack?"

"Yes, Bernstein, the racetrack. Since I was age 21, I have gone to the racetrack once a week and bet everything I have, and every week I win, and win big. It's made me a very, very wealthy man."

Bernstein stares at his friend, stupefied. "Gelderman, I've never heard of such luck."

"It's not luck, my friend," Gelderman whispers as he again furtively peers both ways. "I have a system."

"A system?"

"Yes, my friend, and I want you to have it and use it for your very own. It's your chance for a major comeback."

"Yes, tell me, Gelderman!"

"Well, it's simplicity itself. And it's infallible. Believe it or not, Bernstein, it works every time. Every Thursday, I buy a racing form and I pick a horse. Not just any horse. I study it carefully. I pick a horse. That's every Thursday of my life. Then every Friday of my life, every Friday night I go to synagogue and I pray hard. I keep that racing form in front of me with the name of my horse circled and I keep praying hard. I ask God to let my horse come in. I tell God that I'm putting everything I have on the nose, and to please let that horse come in. I pray to God not to let that horse place or show. He's got to win. Then, every Saturday of my life, I go to the track and put everything I have on that horse. And Bernstein, every Saturday of my life, my prayers are answered."

Bernstein sits there awestruck. "Gelderman, that's fantastic. I just don't know what to say. That's utterly fantastic. What a system. And you say it's infallible?"

"Infallible."

"Well...I just don't know how to thank you. I mean, this is truly my one chance. My one chance to raise myself up again from the dregs of humanity. And Gelderman, I'll owe it all to you. I just will never be able to thank you enough."

"Well, I won't even wish you good luck, Bernstein, you won't even need it."

"Of course, I'm investing my last $60."

"It'll be the start of a new life. God bless! Godspeed! Well...I really must be going, I have several board meetings between now and this evening. So long, my friend."

Gelderman races away in his Silver Cloud, and Bernstein immediately heads for the newsstand to invest in a weekly racing form. Two weeks go by, and it's now a cold and rainy evening, and Gelderman is motoring down the same shabby street. Suddenly he spies his old friend again, this time stooped over, shivering and holding out a tin cup to passersby, barefoot, and with clothes more tattered than ever. His face is ashen white and his eyes are bloodshot as they look up to see the magnificent vehicle once again idling at the curb.

"Bernstein! Bernstein," bellows Gelderman as he lowers his electric window. He leans across the soft, supple leather of the passenger seat and holds out his hand to his old friend, gesticulating in total shock. Bernstein slowly trudges over to the open car window and peers in. Careful to prevent his friend from getting moisture on the English walnut door frame, Gelderman exclaims, "Oy, Bernstein, what has happened?! What has happened?! Look at you! Didn't you follow my system?"

"Yes, Gelderman, I followed your fucking system – and lost everything. I lost my last $60 on one horse. In face, he came in last!"

"Impossible, Bernstein! Impossible! Did you follow my instructions implicitly?"

"Yes, Gelderman, I did just what you told me."

"What synagogue did you go to?"

"B'nai Torah."

"Oy! Schmuck! That's for trotters!"

159. SONG OF SILENCE.

Silverman has earned a reputation among members of his synagogue as somewhat of a high-rolling gambler.

Therefore, it is no surprise to anyone when Silverman comes to a September meeting of the Men's Club and grandly announces that he has a trained parrot that is fully capable of performing as a cantor, and will perform all of the required solo hymns for the forthcoming Rosh Hanashah service, and then a few days later perform the Kol Nidre for Yom Kippur. As he expected, dozens of the members of the Men's Club thought this boast to be uproariously amusing and were willing to place thousands of dollars' worth of bets with Silverman, giving him four to one, five to one and even six to one odds on the Rosh Hanashah service. Silverman took all bets.

Comes Rosh Hanashah eve and the synagogue is packed to the rafters, not merely by pious congregants, but by excited investors. Sure enough, there on the pulpit sits Silverman's parrot, wearing a tiny talis. The shofar is blown and then silence prevails as the audience breathlessly awaits any sound out of the parrot. To their relief, not a sound is heard. Not a single mellow tone is uttered as the little green bird remains perched on the pulpit, motionless and mute. After a few minutes of awkward silence, the embarrassed rabbi asks the real cantor to step forward and perform. A sigh of glee ripples through the audience and all eyes are on Silverman, sitting there in the front row shocked, baffled and about to be many thousands of dollars poorer.

When the ceremony is over, Silverman carries his bird to the parking lot, dumps him on the front seat of the car, climbs in the other side, slams the door and screams, "You fucking bastard! You absolutely screwed me! What a betrayal! We've been working on this secretly and diligently for years. You practiced each one until you knew it by heart, perfectly! You are in beautiful voice! It was going to be a piece of cake! Easy money! You've ruined me! How could you do this to me?"

The bird just sits there and cocks his head, looking at his master. "Squaaaaaawk! Relax, baby, relax! Don't you understand the strategy?"

"What strategy?"

"Wait 'til you see the odds we get for Yom Kippur! Squaaaaaawk!"

160. FOR WHOM THE BELL DOLES.

Quasimodo is in his bell tower in Notre Dame Cathedral. The legendary little hunchback is busily yanking on the bell ropes to ring out the hourly chimes.

But this morning, something notable is to happen. The priest ascends the tower staircase and confronts Quasimodo in the bell chamber. Laying a hand upon his servant's shoulder, the priest says, "Quasimodo, my friend, my son, you've been working faithfully here for quite some time without a break. You deserve a holiday. If you can find a replacement for yourself, take the day off!"

"Oh, Lord in heaven! Oh, Father, my prietht! Thith ith fabulouth. Many, many thankth!"

With that, Quasimodo dashes down the staircase on a dead run and finally emerges through the great doors and out onto the plaza in front of the cathedral. With hysterical joy, he grabs the first bystander he sees and literally drags the protesting man into the cathedral and up the many, many flights of stone steps to the bell tower, unseen by anyone, including the priest who has long since returned to his chambers.

With unbridled glee and superhuman strength, the hunchback raises his victim to his feet and thrusts him against the railing of the bell chamber. Places the first bell rope in the victim's hands as if to demonstrate, Quasimodo helps his new student give a mammoth yank to the rope, sending the massive bronze bell swinging smartly to the opposite side of the chamber. As Quasimodo steps back and folds his arms to observe his student's solo performance, the bewildered victim simply stands there at the rail with a blank stare while the huge bell begins its return sweep through the air. As it does so, it smashes directly into the face of the stupefied victim, knocking him backwards through the air, directly over the stone parapet behind him and out into space, in which he plummets to his doom on the plaza below.

In shock and horror, Quasimodo raises his hands, exclaims, "Oh, my goodneth! What have I done!" and rushes to the parapet to see the culmination of his bell ringing lesson, and the remains of his one-day replacement.

A crowd gathers immediately on the plaza and within minutes can be heard the familiar, "Eeeeeee-yaaaaaaw...eeeeeee-yaaaaaaw" of the French gendarme and the ambulance sirens.

Filled with panic and remorse, Quasimodo scampers down the many flights of stone steps once again and emerges onto the plaza. He elbows his way through the crowd to stare at the crumpled body.

"Quasimodo! Quasimodo! This man fell from your tower! Do you know who he is?" yell members of the crowd.

"Yes, who is he? Who is he?" cry out other bystanders.

"Well, I don't know hith name," says Quasimodo, "but hith fathe rings a bell."

CHAPTER FOURTEEN

GERIATRICKS

Older.Bolder.Better.Wetter.

161. THE TROPHY.

George walks into the Metropolitan Club with a dazzling, curvaceous 25-year-old bimbo on his arm.

As the 85-year-old gentleman and his young friend enter the wood-paneled bar, all conversation stops. All of his friends are awestruck. "Fellas, it gives me great pleasure to introduce to you my new wife, Peaches!"

His group of a dozen friends at the bar are transformed from awe to stupefication. They look at George, they look at his young bride, and they look at each other. Regaining their composure, they lift their glasses high and drink toast after toast.

During the occasion, one of George's friends calls him aside and whispers in his ear, "George, my good friend, we wish nothing but the best for you. She's absolutely a knockout, a bombshell, movie star quality!"

"Thank you, Marshall, that means a lot to me," says George.

"But George, you've got us all buffaloed. I mean...the age spread! It's gigantic! How in the world did you ever land a new bride like this? We're baffled. What's the secret?"

"If you must know," says George, "I lied about my age."

"George! You're 85 years old! What the hell did you tell her?"

"I told her I was 95."

162. ANONYMOUS CALLER.

Gladys Mendelsohn is 91 years old and lives alone.
This evening, the phone rings. She picks it up and says, "Haaallo?"
"Listen, sweetheart…" says an anonymous male voice in husky tones, breathing hard, "I just know that you're waiting there breathlessly for me to hop in my car and come over and race up to your apartment and dash in there and rip all your clothes off and rip all my clothes off and make mad, passionate, steamy, sweaty love. Am I right?"
"You can tell all that from haaallo?"

163. ABLE-BODIED SEMEN.

Seymour is sitting in the doctor's office. He is asked by the urologist to provide a semen sample. His wife Hilda is in the waiting room.

For this humiliating exercise, Seymour is ushered into an adjacent room where he is handed a jar by a nurse and instructed to masturbate and deposit a liberal amount of semen sample into the jar. The nurse closes the door and leaves him alone to his responsibilities.

Thirty minutes go by. Sixty minutes go by. Finally, after one and a half hours, Hilda and the nurse both knock gently on the door. "Seymour...is everything all right in there?"

"Not really," comes the weak reply.

"What's the matter, honey?" calls Hilda.

"Well, I know this is embarrassing," yells Seymour, "but I tried to do it for 30 minutes with my right hand and that was no use. Then I tried for 30 minutes with my left hand and that was no use. Finally, I tried for 30 minutes with both hands. But I still failed to get the cap off this fucking jar."

164. STRATEGIC PRESCRIPTION.

Teitelbaum has asked for an urgent private conference with the doctor.

"Mr. Teitelbaum," says the doctor, "I'm sorry to have to inform you that your wife either has AIDS or Alzheimer's."

"Oh, my Lord," says Teitelbaum, "that's awful! How will I know which it is?"

"Well, here's my recommendation," says the doctor. "This evening, I want you to take her out into the middle of the park. Then I want you to leave her there."

"And then, Doctor?"

"If she finds her way home…don't fuck her."

165. ECONOMY AUDIO.

An elderly gentleman walks into a hearing aid store. The salesman responds by ushering him to an entire wall of glass showcases displaying the latest in the world's hearing aid technology.

"Nowhere, sir, can you find a great range of product selection than here. What can I show you?"

"Well, how much is that model?"

"This, sir, is our super Deluxe Monster Megaphone Model, guaranteed to let the world blast your eardrums out. And it's only $5,800!"

"Let me have a look at something a little less pricey," says the customer.

"Of course, sir. Now, here's a model equipped with such modern technology that it's almost totally invisible to the naked eye. In fact, you have to scratch inside your ear to even relocate it. And it's only $3,995."

"Gee, that's nice, but let me see something more economical."

"Certainly, sir, here's a model that is only $1,295 because of our anniversary sale. It's a real bargain. It usually sells for $2,900."

"Gee, that is a bargain. But let me see perhaps the very lowest-priced hearing aid you have."

"Of course I will. Here's the model. It's a steal at only $25."

"That does sound like a bargain. But wait, that only looks to me like it's a thin piece of wire and a button."

"That's right, sir. That's all it is. The wire goes in your breast pocket and it leads up through the button, which fits nicely into your ear."

"Wow! Does it work?"

"Not really," says the salesman. "But everyone who sees it on you starts speaking louder."

166. THE MIRACLE REMEDY FOR ARTHRITIS.

A very elderly woman hobbles into an arthritis clinic, walking stooped over a cane.

She takes a seat in the reception room, and when her name is called, she hobbles into the doctor's office. Twenty minutes later, she emerges from the doctor's office stately and erect, with perfect posture, wielding a cane with grace and aplomb.

A few of her fellow patients that have seen her come in were still waiting to be called. They look at her with sheer astonishment as she strolls through the waiting room, toward the door.

One woman couldn't contain herself and rose to her feet, hollering to this woman as she was at the door, and said, "Excuse me, ma'am, but I couldn't help noticing this fantastic transformation! I saw you walk in here stooped over, horribly bent and in pain. Now, I see you walk out perfectly erect with absolutely wonderful posture. This doctor must be a miracle-worker!"

"Not exactly," the elderly woman replied. "I'm still in pain. But what he did was to give me a longer cane."

167. WORLD CHAMPION SAMURAI.

CNN is seeking to find the world's greatest samurai.

It sends a reporting and camera team to Tokyo to begin the search. They first go to the famous Kodokan and ask the top sensei there for three recommendations. He first sends the team to the Tokyo suburb of Fuchu. There, they find the home of the eminent Miyuko Sato. He agrees to be interviewed in the garden.

The cameras start rolling. The CNN reporter, on camera, says, "Sato-san, tell us and tell the world audience why you are considered the world's greatest samurai."

"Very simpry this," he says as he unsheathes his giant samurai sword from the scabbard. "Samurai's are judged mostry on the precision accuracy of their swordsmanship."

"Could you demonstrate that for us, sir?" says the reporter.

"I would gradry do so," says the hulking samurai as he doffs his kimono, steps into the garden and spots a delicate butterfly.

In a twinkling, he has lifted the giant sword with a swoosh and goes, "Eeeeeeee-aaaaah!" With that, he severs a wing from the butterfly, stoops down, picks up the wing, turns and smiles sweetly for the camera.

The team continues the interview and leaves. They are impressed, but not entirely convinced. Back to the sensei they go for his second recommendation, which is an introduction to Yaki Takashimaya, an aging samurai nobleman who lives in an imposing country manor house in Shinagawa Prefecture, many miles south of Tokyo. When the CNN team arrives, they are greeted in the imposing doorway by the samurai himself. He is in his eighties, but looking quite physically fit, with a brilliant red kimono and flowing gray hair. After initial pleasantries and few preliminary questions, the team is ushered into his greenhouse, where they view a magnificent collection of bonsai plants.

"Sir, exactly what does it take to become the world's greatest samurai?"

"Far more than rots of ruck," says the samurai with a grin. "Watch this." With that, he reaches into a pot and withdraws one thin blade of grass. He then withdraws his giant samurai sword from its scabbard, doffs his kimono, and places the blade of grass on his lips. As the reporting team holds its breath and as the cameras are rolling, the samurai suddenly puffs the blade of grass up into the air and simultaneously lifts the sword above his head and screams, "Eeeeeee-aaaaah!" And before the blade of grass floats even halfway to the floor, he has neatly severed it down the middle in a precision vertical slice. Once again, the team departs, extremely impressed.

But there is one more samurai that the sensei believes may be the ultimate samurai still alive on the planet. His name is Ishi Muto, who is a 95-year-old farmer living far up on the northern island of Hokkaido. The sensei convinces the team that it would be well worth the trip to meet this man. They charter a plane and make the expedition up to the northerly island.

When they arrive at Ishi's farmhouse, a modest little thatched abode, they are ushered into his living room and provided with tea service.

They start the cameras and the reporters start their interview. Once again, they ask the ultimate questions – what does it take to become the world's greatest samurai?

"That's easy," says Ishi, his wizened, craggy face beaming a radiant smile. "I wir show you!" He doffs his humble cloth kimono and reveals a wrinkle but wiry little body. He unsheathes his sword and stands in the center of the living room. Obviously, he's searching for something. His head bobs from side to side, his eyes darting across the room from one corner to another. Finally, he grins. "Do you see that fry?"

"Yes," says the group in unison, as they wonder what comes next.

"Watch!" says the diminutive samurai, his little beady eyes fixed like radar on the fly as it buzzes across the living room. Ishi's eyes keep tracking the fly as it merrily buzzes from wall to wall. Finally, it is in mid-room and in mid-air. Quickly, he screams, "Eeeeeee-aaaaah!" and his sword whooshes through the air smartly, and he turns to the cameras and bows.

Meanwhile, the fly is still buzzing merrily around the room.

"Ishi-san!" says the announcer with some discomfort and embarrassment, "it was obvious that the fly was your target, but you must admit that the fly is still flying."

"Of course," says Ishi as he stands proudly with his arms folded. "That fry is still frying…but that fry will never fuck again!"

168. EVERYTHING FOR THE MODERN ALTA.

A 94-year-old man and a 92-year-old woman enter Walgreen's in Miami Beach. They demand to see the store manager. After several minutes, the store manager appears and says, "Yes, sir and madam, what can I do for you?"

"Do you carry walkers?" asks the old man.

"Yes, we do, sir."

"And do you carry Depends?"

"We certainly do, sir."

"And Metamucil?"

"Yes, sir, we do."

"And how about bedpans?" asks the woman.

"Yes, we have them, madam."

"And canes, too?"

"Yes, we have a large selection of canes. But tell me, why do you ask?"

"Well, you see, we're getting married next June and we've decided to make your store our bridal registry."

169. THE SIGAFOOS

Three construction workers are sitting together at a lunch break, ruminating about the wonders of the world. One says: Ah wondah what you guys tink am the world's meanest, most viscious animal.?

"Well dat's easy guys," says a second. "De meanest creature evah born am de tigahh! De tigahh am so mean his big fangs can rip yo fuckin' head off with one bite!"

"Dat's true," says the third, "but ah tink dat de absolute meanest meanest animal evah is de alligatah. I mean dose giant jaws wid a million teeth can just clamp on about anyting and snap it in half in one second.!"

"Yeah, dat's true" says the first luncher, nodding in agreement. "But you know guys...ah tink beyond a doubt dat the very meanest creature god ever created on the face of this earth is de sigafoos!"

"De sigafoos???? Sigafoos? What in hell is a sigafoos?" say the other two in unison.

"Well, "says the first, "de sigafoos is about the strangest critter anybody ever saw! He's a very rare animal with a huge slimy body with short fat legs, and he has a huge ugly head on his big shoulders...and another huge ugly head on his ass. He am de most fearsome ting you ever did see!"

"Wait and minute! Wait a minute, pal. Dat's just not possible!! If de sigafoos has a head at one end and a head at his other end, how do he shit??"

"He can't. What de hell do you think makes him so fuckin' mean???"

170. THE PROPOSITION.

In a nursing home, a man dials an inside extension in order to reach a fellow inmate.

"Mrs. Dorfman?" he asks.

"Speaking! Who is this?" she asks.

"This is Mr. Segal," he says. "When I asked you to marry me last night…did you say yes or no?"

"I said yes," she exclaims. "And I'm so glad you called, because I couldn't remember who asked me…"

171. RECOLLECTIONS.

An aging Jew is being interviewed by an American sergeant, following his liberation from a Nazi concentration camp in 1944. "You must've undergone a horrendous experience," says the sergeant. "Sir, please try to describe what it was like there."

"Vell," says the old man, "it vas like notting you could ever imagine."

"Please go ahead, sir," says the sergeant.

"Vell, the whole place had a vall – all round us. It vas ten feet thick. Solid cement. On top of the vall dere was a guard platform every hundred feet. Each guard had a huge machine gun mounted on the platform. Den, every 200 feet, dere vas a search light, a revolving search light that would scan every part of the terrain beyond the vall. Just outside the vall, there vas a moat 30 feet vide. Beyond the moat, dere vas an open field a hundred yards vide in all directions. And beyond the field, dere vas a fence, a huge fence that has barbed vire and was electrified. If you just touched it, it would fry you like an egg. Beyond the fence, there vere patrols with vicious guard dogs that used to cover every inch of the perimeter every 15 minutes."

"That sounds incredible," says the sergeant. "What a place!"

"Yes, it vas," says the old man. "But you know vat? I got in."

172. THE BEACHNIK.

Nussbaum is an 81-year-old widower. He decides to try a nudist colony for the first time. His travel agent sends him to the premier nudist colony on the west coast of Mexico. It is known to have every amenity imaginable, as well as the biggest selection of hot, nude, single women. Nussbaum can't wait to arrive.

Even before he checks in, he eyeballs the beach and is excited to see a free-for-all taking place between dozens and dozens of nude men and women, constituting the most hedonistic Roman orgy he had ever imagined. It is a virtual seaside paradise. Hurriedly, he checks in, goes to his room, removes all of his clothes and quickly heads to the beach.

Almost instantly, he is met by a sultry young lass who grabs him, throws him to the sand and commences to have wild, passionate sex with him.

Following that encounter, he arises totally drained and takes only a few more steps down the beach when he trips and falls in the sand on his stomach. Within three seconds, he is accosted and brutally sodomized by five young, nude, gay men.

Barely surviving that episode, he slowly arises, walks to the hotel elevator, goes immediately to his room, dresses, grabs his luggage and proceeds to the checkout desk.

"But Mr. Nussbaum," says the clerk, "you just arrived an hour ago! Are you checking out already? Is anything wrong?"

"Are you kidding? I couldn't possibly survive the routine here!"

"What do you mean, sir?"

"I mean that I get an erection only once a month...but I fall down five times a day!"

173. TITILLATING TRANSFORMATION.

A 70-year-old man and his 65-year-old wife are walking down a deserted beach together, when poof! – suddenly a genie appears before them.

"Guess what?" says the genie. "It's your lucky day. I'm gonna' grant each of you your fondest wish!"

"How marvelous!" says the wife. "Let me see…oh, I know…my fondest wish is that we are together on a round-the-world cruise!"

"No problem," says the genie. Zap! "Here you are, on the deck of the new Queen Mary!"

"Oh, boy," says the husband, "and I get to go along for the ride! Okay, now my wish is that I'm on this ship with a companion 20 years younger than me."

"Okay, no problem," says the genie. Zap! "You're 85!"

174. LUXURIOUS LISTENING.

An 87-year-old man walks into a very posh hearing aid store on Rodeo Drive in Beverly Hills. He asks for the absolute top-of-the-line in high-tech hearing aids. He spends thousands of dollars, but is confident that he has the best as he walks out.

A week later, he's back in the store for a small adjustment in the frequency of the device. "Well, how is it working?" asks the same clerk.

"Absolutely marvelous," says the man. "It works like a charm, just as advertised. I can hear everything perfectly."

"That's wonderful," says the clerk. "I'll bet your family is very pleased. After all, you were almost stone deaf when you came here, and this purchase seemed to make all the difference!"

"Well, frankly," says the customer, "I haven't told my family yet."

"You haven't told them yet? Why not?"

"Because every evening, I sit there at the dinner table and listen to the family conversation. And I've changed my will three times."

175. BEATING THE HMO.

An aging couple in Oklahoma goes to a sex therapist. The doctor asks, "What can I do for you?"

The man says, "Will you watch us have sexual intercourse?"

The doctor is dubious, but he is so amazed that such an elderly couple is asking for sexual advice that he agrees.

When the couple finishes, the doctor says, "There's absolutely nothing wrong with the way you have intercourse." He thanks them for coming, he wishes them good luck, he charges them $50 and he says good-bye.

The next week, however, the couple returns and asks the sex therapist to watch again. The sex therapist is a bit puzzled, but agrees.

This happens several weeks in a row. The couple makes an appointment, they have intercourse with no problems, pay the doctor and then leave.

Finally, after five or six weeks of this routine, the doctor says, "I'm sorry, but I have to ask. Just what are you trying to find out?"

The old man says, "We're not trying to find out anything. She's married and we can't go to her house. I'm married and we can't go to my house. The Holiday Inn charges $98. The Hilton charges $139. We do it here for $50, and I get $43 back from Medicare."

176. THE GIFT THAT KEEPS GIVING.

For Saul's 85th birthday, his friends all get together and decide to send him a 25-year-old blonde for the evening.

She knocks on his apartment door, he opens it, and she stands there with her arms spread, her body wrapped in a big red ribbon with a bow. "Good evening, Mr. Dorfman. Your friends all got together and sent me here to wish you a happy 85th birthday and offer you super sex!"

The gentleman pauses for a moment and sighs, looks longingly at her lissome figure and replies, "I think I'll take the soup."

177. TRIPLE DEMENTIA.

Three senior citizens in their upper eighties are sharing a comfortable house at the south end of Miami Beach.

As usual, this afternoon all three men are in their living room easy chairs reading the latest news. Suddenly Abe gets up and says, "Fellas, I'm going up to take a shower." Two minutes later, a voice is heard from the second floor, saying, "Fellas, am I on the way up to take a shower or have I already taken a shower?"

The other two reply in unison, "Abe, of course not. You haven't taken a shower. You're going to take a shower. Go take your shower, Abe!"

A half an hour later, Max says to Jake, "Jake, maybe you'd better go up and check on Abe and see how he's doing."

Jake arises and gets halfway up the staircase when he yells back to Max, "Max, did I already check on Abe or am I on my way to check on Abe?"

"Jake! For God's sake, you're on your way up to check on Abe. Keep going! Keep going! You haven't gotten there yet!" Max laments. He thereupon throws his hands in the air, shakes his head sadly and whispers to himself, "Oy vay!" and begins to rap his knuckles several times on the coffee table in front of him while he exclaims to himself, "Wow! Am I glad my mind is still in one piece. Hey! Is that the front door or the back door?"

178. ANNIVERSAY SCHMALTZ.

Simon and Sophie are celebrating their 40th wedding anniversary. For the celebration, the couple decides to return to the place where it all began – the Bridal Suite of the Waldorf. After cocktails and a romantic dinner served in the room, they prepare for bedtime. He dons a brand new bathrobe, and she repairs to the bathroom where she attires herself in none other than the thin black negligee she wore on their original wedding night.

Reappearing gradually in the bedroom, Sophie says coyly, "Simon, look what I'm wearing – the very same black negligee I wore on our wedding night."

"Hmmmnnn," he mutters, apparently unmoved.

"Simon," she continues, "tell me, darling, what were you thinking that first night when you saw me in this?"

"I recall it well. I was thinking that I'm going to spend a lifetime sucking your tits until they're dry and withered, and fucking your brains out."

"And what are you thinking now, Simon?"

"I'm thinking that I did a hell of a job."

179. VITAL STATISTICS.

A gentleman undergoes a complete physical examination and then takes a seat in the reception room to await the findings of the doctor. Finally, the doctor emerges and asks him to step into his office for consultation.

"Mr. Green," says the doctor, "you are in marvelous health. In fact, in my opinion, you are a first-class specimen of a 65-year-old man."

"Doctor, did I say I was 65? I'm 75."

"Seventy-five! That's incredible!" says the doctor. "Please sit down, Mr. Green. This is really one for the books. I've got to get your family history!" The doctor picks up a pen and pad and begins to write furiously. "Now, tell me, Mr. Green, at what age did your father die?"

"Did I say my father died? My father's very much alive today. He's 95, hale and hearty, going strong. In fact, he jogs three miles a day and swims 20 laps in the pool ever morning. He's in terrific shape."

"That's fantastic!" says the doctor, continuing to write furiously. "Now, tell me, Mr. Green, at what age did your grandfather die and from what disease?"

"Doctor, did I say my grandfather is dead? My grandfather is 115 today and is as strong as an ox. He plays three rounds of golf each week. He even dates. In fact, Doctor, I'll have you know that in two weeks, my grandfather is getting married!"

The doctor lays down his pen. "Married? Your grandfather's getting married? Now, you must be putting me on, Mr. Green. That simply defies credibility. Why in the world would a 115- year-old man want to get married?"

"Doctor, did I say he WANTED to get married?"

180. PREPPING FOR THE BIG EVENT.

Blanche is an 80-year-old widow and has been courted for years by Myron, an 81-year-old widower.

Finally, Myron wins her heart and she consents to marriage. A big wedding is held, all of their friends and family attend, and now they are alone on their wedding night. They each prepare for the matrimonial bed. Myron showers and shaves and applies his best cologne and then dons his niftiest bathrobe. Blanche goes through her own preparations, emerges in an elegant negligee, turns the lights down low, turns on the hi-fi system and gets into bed. Nervously, Myron removes his robe, removes his shorts and enters his side of the bed. The moment for the consummation of the marriage is at hand.

As Myron begins to kiss and fondle his bride, Blanche whispers into his ear with a sultry voice, "Myron, you won't forget to put on a condom, will you?"

"A condom? A condom, Blanche? You want me to wear a condom?"

"Yes, Myron, please, a condom."

"But Blanche, you're 80 years old. I really don't think you have to worry about pregnancy."

"Myron, I'm not worried at all about pregnancy. It's just that the moisture is bad for my arthritis!"

181. ADVANCED BRIDAL SELECTION.

Seymour is visiting his 85-year-old father who is presently living at one of those famous, luxurious retirement communities in Southern California.

Shortly after his son's arrival and with cocktails poured, the father exclaims, "Well, I have big news, my son. I'm getting married again!"

"Gee, Dad, I think that's marvelous! In all these years since Mother died, I've been hoping you'd find someone who's the right one for you!"

"Well, I have, Son, and she's perfect for me."

"Boy, Dad, that's great! I'll bet she's beautiful!"

"Well, not really. In fact, she's kind of homely."

"Well, then, I'll bet she's young and shapely, isn't she?"

"No, Son, not really. In fact, she's a little older than I am and on the heavy side."

"Well then, Dad, she must be brilliant!"

"No, Seymour, I hate to disappoint you, but she somewhat on the dull side."

"Gee, Dad, if she isn't beautiful or young or brilliant, why are you marrying her?"

"She can still drive at night."

182. REJUVENATION.

Hyman is sitting in his doctor's examining room, up on the table, stark naked. He has just completed an examination.

"Doctor, I just have one more thing to ask. It's been really puzzling me for quite a while."

"What is it, Mr. Hyman?"

"Well, Doctor, ten years ago when I was 50, I could grasp my erection with both hands and, no matter how hard I tried, I couldn't bend it. Nowadays, Doctor, I can take my two hands and bend it over like a pretzel!"

"So?"

"Well, Doctor, could it be that my hands are becoming that much stronger?"

183. DÉJÀ VU.

Mrs. Berkowitz meets Mr. Siegel at an upstate New York resort and tries her best to turn on the heavy charm.

She finally has him cornered in the cocktail lounge one evening, and after several hours of conversation, she squints across the candle-lit table and says to her aging prey, "You know something, Mr. Siegel? You look very much like my third husband."

In response, Mr. Siegel looks across the table at Mrs. Berkowitz and says, "Gee, Mrs. Berkowitz, I had no idea you had been married three times."

"I haven't, Mr. Siegel – only twice."

184. THE AVID AMPHIBIAN.

An elderly gentleman is strolling by a pond in the park one day. Suddenly, he hears a tiny voice emanating from the edge of the pond, and it is chirping, "Pssssst...pick me up! Pick me up!"

The old man stops, turns and spies a little green frog sitting on a lily pad at the end of the pond. With some curiosity, he goes over, stoops and lifts the frog up gently in his hand. He brings the frog to eye level. "Now kiss me," whispers the frog," and I'll turn into a beautiful princess."

The old man ponders the situation for a moment and then quickly stashes the frog in his coat pocket and strolls on.

"Hey! Hey! Let me out! Let me out!" chirps the frog from the pocket.

With some irritation, the old man lifts the frog from his pocket and brings him back to eye level. "What is it?" he asks.

"Don't you understand?" chirps the frog in desperation. "I said kiss me and I'll turn into a beautiful princess!"

As the old man strolls on and calmly places the frog back in his pocket, he murmurs, "I know, I know, I heard, but at my age, I think I'd rather have a talking frog."

185. THE CERTIFICATION.

It has now been several weeks since Max Plotkin's triple bypass. He's feeling fit as a fiddle and raring to go. Every night when he climbs in bed and is ready to climb onto Sarah, she puts up her guard like a prizefighter and states categorically, "Max, nothing doing. Nothing doing. I'm not letting you lay a finger on me until you're in absolutely perfect shape. A full recuperation." This scene goes on nightly for several weeks, until finally Max asks plaintively, "What can I possibly do to prove that I'm okay?"

"Max, I won't even consider you recuperated until you get a note from the doctor!"

The following day, Plotkin is in the office of his cardiologist, pleading his case. "Morris, would you believe it? Sarah won't let me touch her until I get a signed and sealed note from you. So go ahead, look me over and stamp me Grade A."

Morris the cardiologist gives him the works and, upon completion of the examination, pronounces Plotkin in perfect shape. He goes to his desk, sits down, takes a sheet of his person stationery and writes as follows:

> "This is to attest that Max Plotkin is as strong as an ox, as healthy as a bull, and as virile as a three-year-old stallion. He is a prime specimen of American manhood.
> Signed: Morris Ginsburg, MD, Cardiologist"

He returns to Plotkin, smiles and hands him the sheet of stationery. In the process of dressing, Plotkin excitedly grabs the sheet and reads it.

"Hmmmmm...Hmmmmmmnnn," Plotkin murmurs. "Not bad, Morris. Not bad at all. It reads quite well. Could I simply request one small addition?"

"What's that, Max?"

"Morris, would you mind writing at the top of the sheet: TO WHOM IT MAY CONCERN?"

186. THE VISION.

Mr. Levine, a widower, meets Mrs. Epstein, a widow, on the beach of the Eden Rock Hotel, Miami Beach. They feel an immediate magnetic attraction to each other and strike up a lively conversation in which they each divulge a lifetime of history of joys and sorrows. It seems like a match made in heaven.

The romantic interlude then takes the couple into the water, wading out until they are both knee deep in the calm, sultry waters of the Atlantic. The conversation between the couple grows increasingly intimate, and before they know it, a half hour has passed.

At last, Mr. Levine gazes into Mrs. Epstein's limpid brown eyes and says, "You know, Mrs. Epstein, a wonderful thought just occurred to me. What would you think if you and I went back on the beach and got dried off and then we want back up to my suite in our bathrobes and we put some nice Montovani music on my quadraphonic hi-fi system, and then we turned the lights down low and then we ordered room service? We could order a nice bottle of champagne on ice and shrimp cocktail and some caviar and crackers or maybe some smoked salmon. And then maybe later, Mrs. Epstein, we could get up and have a little dance together around the living room, and I could hold you close, and then I would waltz you into the bedroom, and we would pull down the shades, and then…"

"Yes, Mr. Levine, yes, that sounds wonderful…but do you think maybe we could move out a little further into the water so nobody can see what we're talking about?"

CHAPTER FIFTEEN

AFTERLIFE

Getting To Heaven Isn't Rocket Séance.

187. WHAT A WAY TO GO.

The funeral of one of New York's most prominent cardiologists is taking place at St. Patrick's cathedral.

All of East Side society turns out to pay its respects.

The funeral is rather straightforward and conventional, until the final moment when, after a priestly benediction, a curtain is drawn on center stage to reveal a mammoth plastic heart. The organ music blares, the casket is slowly closed, and to the astonishment of the audience, the casket begins to move on special tracks through an electronic pulley, slowly pulled toward the heart. At that moment, the great heart splits in two and its two sides open wide as the casket begins to slowly move within it. After the casket is well within the heart, the two sides gradually close together once again, and the reconstituted heart, ablaze in spotlights, is all that is visible.

The audience gasps in amazement and appreciation.

However, the reverie of the worshippers is interrupted by hysterical laughter from a gentleman seated in the first row, who falls off his chair and begins rolling around the floor, holding his sides. The persons in his row are stunned to see and hear this, and one of them says, "Sir! What on Earth are you doing? Don't you realize you're at a funeral?" in a loud whispers.

"Yes, I do," says the man from the floor, still convulsed in laughter and with tears running down his cheeks. "I'm really sorry. But I couldn't help imagining my own funeral. I'm a gynecologist."

188. HELL TO PAY.

Melvin Feinberg walks into St. Peter's reception room and asks for admittance.

The receptionist informs him that St. Peter is busy, but that she'll check his pre-qualifications. A few minutes later, she comes back and says, "Mr. Feinberg, as you know, we only accept exceptional people here at this level. Our database does not show anything in terms of notable achievements of yours. Is there anything noteworthy that you've accomplished there on Earth?"

"Well," says Feinberg, "history will show that I was the first man of my religious preference to ever rape the headmistress of Hell's Angels on the beach at Malibu in front of 4,000 screaming members, who were attending the Hell's Angels National Convention."

"That's an amazing stunt," says the receptionist. "But somehow, I don't seem to find it here in our database. When did this incident happen?"

"About three minutes ago."

189. PLAYING SUDDEN DEATH.

Gelderman's drive off the tee takes a terrific slice and he ends up in the rough. Being a champion golfer, he is quite perturbed at himself, but yet confident that he can extricate from this predicament. Standing there in the weeds, he takes a four-iron, carefully swings back, whacks it hard, and lo and behold, it veers off-course into a large oak tree just 20 feet from him and rebounds directly back to him, hitting him squarely in the forehead and killing him.

He's now at St. Peter's office for his reception discussion.

St. Peter scans the computer printout. "Well, well, well, Mr. Gelderman, I see that you are something of a champion golfer. Is that true?"

"Well, I got here in two, didn't I?"

190. CANNY CORTEGE.

A funeral procession is coming down Main Street. It is led by two glistening black hearses. Those are followed by the widow, dressed in black. A few paces behind her is walking a pit bull, and a few paces behind the pit bull are 200 women in single file, marching solemnly

Witnessing this parade, a young woman is stupefied. She runs from the curb out onto the street and begins to walk alongside the widow. "Please forgive me, madam, for disturbing you in this solemn hour," the young woman says, "but I've never seen a procession like this. Who are in those hearses?"

"Well, if you must know," the widow says, "in the first hearse is my late husband, who happens to be a real bastard. In the second hearse is my late mother-in-law, who happens to be a real bitch."

"And how did they die?"

"Well,' said the widow, "they were both attacked and killed by this pit bull."

The woman ponders that one for a moment and then asks, "Say, you know what? Would it be at all possible that I could borrow that pit bull?"

"Get in line."

191. PARADISE FOUND.

A Palestinian terrorist blows himself up.

Within minutes, he finds himself in St. Peter's reception room. "Good evening, my friend. We've been expecting you," says St. Peter.

Omar is elated. "And where is Paradise?"

"Right through that door," points St. Peter.

Omar dashes through the door, takes two steps beyond it, and is immediately leaped upon, stripped, beaten and sodomized by George Washington, John Adams, James Madison and Thomas Jefferson and their friends. An hour later, he staggers back through the door to St. Peter and says, "Wait a minute! Wait a minute! They promised me 72 virgins up here!"

"Schmuck!" says St. Peter. "You didn't listen! They promised you 72 Virginians!"

192. GETTING AHEAD.

Norman Levinson passes away and now is beautifully dressed, reclining in his casket. On the morning of the funeral, Mrs. Levinson visits the funeral parlor to be sure that all is in readiness for the afternoon services. She looks at her late husband laying there and is horrified. She calls for the funeral director, who appears on the run. "What's wrong, Mrs. Levinson?"

"Guess what?" she says. "I forgot to tell you something very, very important. Norman had always asked to be buried in his blue suit, and your embalmer dressed him in his gray herringbone! This is just totally unacceptable! He's got to be changed."

"Right away, Mrs. Levinson," the funeral director replies and heads back to his office to make arrangements.

"But Harry!" says his assistant back in the office, "You know very well that the funeral is scheduled to begin in a few minutes and there's no way on Earth that we can get across town to Mr. Levinson's home, retrieve his blue suit from the closet and bring it back here to redress him. It's impossible!"

"You're right, my boy, you're right," says funeral director Harry, "but wait…I think I have a plan."

"Where are you going, Harry?" asks the assistant.

"The deceased who is already here awaiting the 4 p.m. funeral has a blue suit. I'm gonna' use that one. I'll get Norman dressed right away."

"But Harry, there just isn't time. The guests are gonna' arrive any minute now! But wait! I think that I have an even better plan."

Having total confidence is his able and resourceful assistant, Harry shrugs his shoulders and walks back to reassure Mrs. Levinson. Minutes later, as the mourners file into the funeral home and enter the sanctuary, Norman Levinson is indeed miraculously resplendent in a blue suit. The ultra-fine blue flannel, double-breasted look goes perfectly with his new complexion.

Mrs. Levinson and family file past the casket, look at the late husband and father and uncle with tenderness and awe and admiration for his sartorial radiance.

Meanwhile, in the back of the hall, Harry grabs his assistant and says, "Hey, that's amazing. That's really amazing! You did it! You did it! He's dressed beautifully in that blue double-breasted suit owned by the 4:00 guy! But wait a minute! That was an impossible feat! Even Houdini couldn't have pulled that off. How did you do it?"

"Harry," he whispers, "it was easy. I just switched heads."

193. THE FEMALE IMPERATIVE.

St. Peter is welcoming his latest group of 500 male applicants. "Okay, you guys, I want you to shape up. I want all those men thoroughly dominated by their wives to get in this line and stand over here, and I want all others in that line."

After much consternation and chaos and shuffling, he finds that the line of dominated husbands numbers 499. He turns to the single gentleman in the other line and goes up to him. "Tell me what caused you to stand in this line, my friend," St. Peter says.

"My wife told me to."

194. THE HOLY TAXI.

St. Peter is interviewing a number of new recruits. He comes to one who is obviously a Pakistani and says to him, "Sir, exactly what do you think qualifies you to be up here?"

The young man smiles and says, "On Earth, I was a taxi driver and drove a very holy cab. My whole life, I drove a holy cab."

"And just why do you think your cab was holy?"

"Because every single passenger who got in immediately started praying."

195. JUST ONE SNIFF.

Schwartz is terminally ill and the hospital decided it can do no more for him. He is now home in his own bedroom in his very own bed, with his family gathered around him.

As he lies there on the silk sheets contemplating his final hours, his nostrils suddenly quiver at the increasingly strong aroma wafting up the stairway from the kitchen.

"David," calls Schwartz. "David, come quickly. David, I need you."

"What is it, Poppa? What is it? What can I do for you?" his loyal 16-year-old son asks.

"David, what is that I smell? What is that marvelous aroma? Could that be, could it really be the fabulous mandelbread baked by my wife Sadie, your wonderful mother?"

Schwartz's nostrils are now quivering violently. "Oy, oy! Yes, yes, it must be. That's the mandelbread I love."

"David, mein son, come closer," Schwartz mutters. His son hovers over him.

"Yes, Poppa. What can I do? What can I do?"

"David, I haven't got much time left. Before I go, quick, run downstairs and get me a plate of that wonderful mandelbread!"

Dutifully, his son races down the stairs.

Two minutes later, David returns empty-handed.

"David! What's the matter? Where's my mandelbread?" Schwartz asks.

"I'm sorry, Poppa. I'm terribly sorry, but Mamma says you can't have any."

"Why not!"

"Mamma says it's for the shiva."

196. A TISKET, A CASKET.

Perlman dies, leaving dozens and dozens of creditors holding the bag. He is hundreds of thousands of dollars in debt. Now that he's gone, chances look very slim for the creditors.

It is now the day of his funeral, and the many dozens of his creditors are filing past his open casket. Perlman is laying there, dressed in his Sunday best, looking magnificent, belying the impecunious state of his estate.

One of his creditors is especially bitter. As he passed the open casket, he leans over and places his mouth an inch from Perlman's ear and whispers, "Perlman, you cock-sucking son of a bitch. You miserable bastard. You owe me 90,000 fucking dollars and you went and took the easy way out. Now you're gone and I am left with nothing but your lousy IOU. Well, maybe you got away with it, you fucker, but at least I'll have the satisfaction of cutting your balls off!"

With that, the creditor unobtrusively pulls out a straight razor and unzips the fly of the corpse. Suddenly, one eye of the corpse pops open and he is heard to whisper, "You, I'll pay."

197. ALMOST IMMORTALITY.

Mrs. Lipschitz is speaking to God and pleading for immortality. "Please, God, what do I have to do to achieve it? I'll do anything." Day after day, month after month she keeps asking. She's obsessed with the quest.

One day in a fit of impatience, God says to her, "Okay, Mrs. Lipschitz, okay, I'll tell you what. You can have immortality, but you have to earn it. You have to lead a saintly life, an impeccable life, a life thoroughly above reproach, then maybe…just maybe I'll grant you immortality."

Mrs. Lipschitz is thrilled beyond words. She dedicates herself to this quest. She lives her life for others, she gives money to every conceivable cause, she helps blind people across the street, she cooks mightily for bake sales at the Hadassah, she sits on dozens of benefit committees and is chairperson on five of them. She truly leads a pristine life.

Now she is in her mid-sixties and she's speaking to God again. "Well, God, what do you think? Have I done it? Have I done enough? I do everything for everybody. Haven't I earned it? Haven't I earned immortality?"

Tired of the whole subject by now, God says, "All right, Mrs. Lipschitz, all right, you've done it. I'm going to give you immortality."

Mrs. Lipschitz is supremely elated. She sits there alone in her bedroom, almost bursting with joy. Suddenly she says to herself, "Well, if I'm going to live forever, I better look the part!" The next morning, she rushes to Elizabeth Arden and has a complete makeover. She is Chaneled from head to foot. Then she rushes to New York's top cosmetic surgeon and has a complete facelift. Every wrinkle is removed. She has a complete hair makeover, including style and color. Finally, Mrs. Lipschitz emerges – brand new.

One day later, she is crossing Madison Avenue and is hit by a truck. She is killed instantly. Now she's in the reception room in Heaven and God happens to walk by. "God! God!" she cries. "It's me! It's me! Mrs. Lipschitz! Remember? You gave me immortality, and then yesterday you had me hit by a truck and killed! How could you do this?"

"Mrs. Lipschitz? Is that you, Mrs. Lipschitz? Oh, I'm so sorry! I'm so terribly sorry! I didn't recognize you!"

198. SICK STORY.

Three recently deceased young ladies are sitting in the reception room in Heaven, awaiting consultation with St. Peter. Finally, he appears and commences the interviews.

"Good morning, Ms. Violet. Let me welcome you here. Tell me, please, what was your cause of death?"

She ponders for a moment and then says, "Ah'm not sure, St. Pete, but as ah recollect, ah believe it was a disease starting with the letter C."

"Oh, perhaps that was cancer?"

"Yas, suh, dat's it, cansuh."

He turns to the next young lady and offers the same welcome and the same question. "Well, suh," Hyacinth replies, "ah don't recall xactly, but ah believe it started with the letter P."

"Hmmmn. Could that have been p-pneumonia, Hyacinth?"

"Why, yas, suh, dat's it."

Then St. Peter turns to the third lady and inquires as to her cause of death. "St. Pete, ah don't rightly remember, but I think it started with the letter G."

"Well, let's see. Could that have been gonorrhea?"

"Yas, suh, ah definitely recall now dat was it."

"But wait a minute," St. Peter interjects. "Gonorrhea isn't fatal."

"It is if you give it to Big Leroy."

199. ALL-STAR CAST.

Cecil B. DeMille is ushered into the reception room in Heaven. St. Peter rushes up to him and throws his arms around the director in a fit of hysterical glee.

"CB! CB! You're finally here! You just don't know how anxiously we've been awaiting your arrival!"

Obviously flattered, DeMille bows graciously and says, "Why thank you, Peter, thank you. It's very good to be here."

"You don't understand how exciting it is for us to finally have you, CB," St. Peter exclaims. "We've all been waiting to have you arrive so that we can finally have you direct the ultimate film of the universe. I mean, just think of it. You can pick any of the greats throughout the history of world cinema, any of the legendary actors and actresses that have passed on to us, history's finest cinematographers, makeup artists, special effects artists, writers, musicians, sound effects technicians. Think of it, CB. You can select the all-star cast of the universe!"

"I can?" CB responds. "Anyone? Any of the great talents in history? They're all here for me to pick and choose?"

"Yes, CB, anyone."

DeMille begins to pace the reception room floor nervously. "Oh my, this is terribly exciting. I never contemplated this. Let me see now, let me see. I think I'll have John Huston assist me, and I think I'll select John Barrymore as my leading man – no, wait, I think I'll make it Rudolph Valentino. Then maybe Clara Bow as my female lead, or maybe Theda Bara. And let's see, who should I choose as my ingénue? Maybe …maybe…"

"Wait a minute, CB, wait a minute. Hold on. I'm terribly sorry, but that part's taken," St. Peter whispers.

"Taken? It's already taken?" exclaims DeMille.

"Yes, CB, I'm sorry. I forgot to mention…it seems that God has this friend…"

READ AT YOUR OWN RISQUE!

200. THE SÉANCE.

It has now been a year since Nathan Mendelsohn dropped dead. His wife Gertrude is now desperately trying to reach him.

She's desperate enough that she hires a local medium for $750 in an effort to establish communication with her late husband.

She's now sitting in an inner chamber of the medium's apartment, which is draped with velvet and features a small Egyptian table at the center. Gertrude Mendelsohn sits in the pitch dark room across the table from the medium.

"Nathan Mendelsohn. Nathan Mendelsohn! Can you hear us?" murmurs the medium.

"Nathan Mendelsohn. Wherever you are, speak to us," says the medium in the darkness.

There is nothing but silence. The medium speaks again. "Nathan Mendelsohn, wherever you are, speak to us."

Gertrude sits on the edge of her chair with bated breath.

The room is hushed. All of a sudden, from somewhere unrecognizable, comes a voice, "Hello?"

"What was that?" exclaims Gertrude excitedly.

"Hello?" says the distant voice once again.

"Oh, my God! Nathan? Nathan? Is that you?" Gertrude screams.

"Gertrude? Gertrude? Is that you?"

"Oh, my God! It's Nathan! It really is Nathan! Nathan! Is that really you?"

"Yes, Gertrude, it's really me. I'm really here."

"Oy! This is incredible. This is so exciting! Nathan! Nathan, tell me…are you all right? Are you okay?"

"Yes, darlink! Yes, darlink! I'm fine. I'm feeling just fine. How are you?"

"I'm fine, Nathan. But tell me, what's happening to you? What do you do all day wherever you are?"

"What do I do all day? It's great. It's simply great here. I get up in the morning, I get fed, and then I'm fucking for two hours. Then I get fed some more, then I'm fucking for a couple more hours, then I rest, then I'm fucking for another hour or two, then I get fed, then I go to sleep!"

"What? What? Nathan? You? That's incredible! That's marvelous! What a life! You just love it up there in Heaven!"

"Gertrude, who's in Heaven? I'm a bull in Montana."